The Nightingale Sings

Anne Crowley

With Tammy Mal

Copyright © 2016 Anne Crowley

All rights reserved.

ISBN: 1537621920
ISBN-13: 978-1537621920

This book is dedicated to Andrew Crowley

For his ever-loving support

ACKNOWLEDGMENTS

With much gratitude to my friend and fellow author Tammy O'Reilly for her unending, unfailing support and her endless patience. Thank you Tammy, and God Bless your future endeavors.

My thanks to Andrew who has always been there with his constant optimism.

Anne Crowley

AUTHOR'S NOTE

It appears to me that my advanced age allows me the privilege of telling my story. From the lessons learned in the living, what is most outstanding is the love I've been privileged to share, and in that loving, the many joys of that love, the children, and grandchildren.

While one is in the process of living, one can recognize the hand which has done the weaving of the fibers that complete the final tapestry, and though the sins of the fathers may continue, so, too, do the many characteristics which comprise one generation to the next.

From my vantage point, the importance of the love stories and the fruits of those loves are what matter. At times, reliving some of the heart-wrenching experiences was a deterrent, but finally, I felt the compulsion to compile this story of my life.

Anne Coar Crowley
September 11, 2016

Anne Crowley

PROLOGUE

It was August 31, 1980, a sweltering hot night on Lewis Lake in the small town of Union Dale, Pennsylvania, and I could not sleep. Earlier that evening, my husband, Stan and I had had one of the most terrible arguments of our married life. It had to do with money and the fact that we were unable to financially help our oldest daughter, Anne and her husband, Tom Hodgins. Stan had gone to bed early, a rarity for him as he always stayed up until midnight, but I could not sleep.

I paced around the cottage, our summer retreat, and tried to read but my mind would not settle. The heat of the day had brewed up a thunderstorm, and I stared out at the lake, listening to the thunder rumbling in the distance. I kept telling myself that I needed to go to bed because we had a busy day the next day. Anne and Tom were taking us out for our anniversary and also to celebrate the birthday of our youngest son, Stanley Jr, nicknamed Chopper.

Finally, around 1:00 a.m. I crawled into bed and was just dozing off when a bolt of lightning struck so close to the cottage that it rattled the windows. I leaped out of the bed with a terrifying thought; "Something has happened to one of my children!"

I had no idea why that thought popped into my mind, but I couldn't shake the feeling of distress that engulfed me. Rushing upstairs, I checked on my three youngsters, each sleeping soundly, and tried to assure myself that everyone was okay. The feeling of distress persisted, however, and I was unable to explain it.

I was still awake at 3:00 a.m. but I must have dozed off again because the next thing I knew, the shrill ringing of the phone startled me awake. Bleary-eyed, I glanced at the clock which read 4:05 a.m. and thought, "I'm not on call; why is the phone ringing at four in the morning?"

Stan was still asleep, and I jumped out of bed intent on grabbing the phone before it woke him. Although I wasn't on call—I worked in the medical profession—when I answered the phone, I found an ICU nurse from St. Joseph's Hospital on the other end.

"Mrs. Coar, I've just had a call from a Mrs. Nelson who's trying to get in touch with you; something about a shooting and your daughter. Here's her number, call her."

Mrs. Nelson was Ann Nelson, my son-in-law, Tom Hodgins' mother. I immediately called her, and remember feeling abject terror when her first words were, "Are you sitting down?"

Although the phone call is foggy, I remember Ann Nelson informing me that there had been a shooting and that our oldest daughter, Anne, had "shot herself in the head."

I don't know what kind of noise came from me, but my husband was immediately beside me, grabbing the phone. It was Stan who got the particulars from Ann Nelson. The shooting had occurred in Scranton, at the couple's apartment at 606 Clay Avenue.

"Anne and Tom were quarreling," Ann Nelson said, "And Anne took Tom's gun, and shot herself in the head."

According to her, Anne was still alive, but unconscious in the emergency room. We called our second oldest daughter, Cathy, who had just given birth to her second child, Kelly, and asked that she come to the cottage to tend to the children.

With that done, Stan and I quickly got ready to go. I remember standing in the doorway of the closet trying to think of how to get dressed and finally grabbing a two-piece pantsuit and putting it on without underwear. I wasn't thinking clearly; I was in shock.

The hospital was located twenty-five miles away—the longest trip of mine or Stan's life. As the miles passed by, my only thought was "Please, Dear Lord, let me see her alive once more," and, "What's going to happen to her daughter, Amy?"

CHAPTER ONE

Had anyone told me in my childhood of the suffering and pain I would endure during my life, I would not have believed them. I was born on Thursday, January 1, 1931, at St. Joseph's Hospital, in the midst of a howling blizzard, the third of four children. I was the only child of Francis and Alberta Walsh born in a hospital, the others being home-birthed, as was the custom then. My mother swore that she'd never go to the hospital again, and she didn't, not until her sixty-fifth year.

My father, Francis P. Walsh, was born on February 28, 1901, in Forest City, Pennsylvania, the fourth child and third son of Michael and Anna Connolly Walsh. "Pop's" parents had emigrated from Ireland to Philadelphia; Michael in 1882 and Anna arriving in Boston in 1880. They married in Forest City on January 20, 1892, and went on to have six children: James, Joseph, Agnes, Francis, (my dad), Alice, and Mary.

My father, (Pop), was a tall, lean man with gray hair and blue eyes, a wonderful sense of humor, and poor health—the result of working in the mines as a breaker boy at age twelve—from his twenties to the end of his days. He attended school only to the eighth grade—for not until 1916 was a law passed requiring children to attend school until age 16—but he was a very intelligent man. In his youth, he suffered a spontaneous pneumothorax due to a bleb and was sent home from the University of Pennsylvania Hospital to "eat, drink and be merry," for, doctors said, he would be dead in three months. Although he proved them wrong by living another twenty-five years, he continuously suffered from some type of lung infection—bronchitis, pneumonia, and eventually, tuberculosis

My mother, Anna, was born to James and Honora (Daven) Connolly who were married in Ireland and migrated to Boston with their children, Festus, Anna, (my mother), Sarah, and Thomas in 1880. They had an older son as well, Martin who would also immigrate in 1884. Later, James and Nora would add three more children to their growing brood: Mary, John and adopted daughter, Susan.

Upon arriving in America, James and Nora stayed with the family of Festus Kane, a not uncommon practice, for immigrants had to be sponsored, be in good health and have thirty dollars in their pocket when they came to America. Later, they moved to Minooka and the story in the family is that it took James six days to walk there with the cow! Today, Minooka is less than an hour drive by car.

On February 22, 1922, my parents were married in St. Agnes Church, Forest City by Reverend Manley. It was not a big affair, however, as there was a great deal of prejudice among the Irish marrying outside of the nationality, especially to ethnic Europeans, of which my mother was one. My mother never truly felt that Ma and Pa Walsh accepted her, and Pop, with his ill health, never attained the financial success that his brothers and sisters did. Pa

Walsh was the co-founder of the M.J. Walsh Insurance Company, now operated by his great-grandson, James Fitzsimmons and renamed the Fitzsimmons Agency. Pa was also the Constable in the town, and a volunteer firefighter.

Pa Walsh, a tall, lean and stern, white-haired man, was never affectionate with us, and we rarely visited our paternal grandparents. In fact, I remember only one family dinner with the Walsh, Fitzsimmons, and Burns cousins. At that time, Pa held my cousin, Betty Burns, on his lap and gave her money—but none to the rest of us. My Grandparents never came to our home either. Apparently unhappy with my father's choice of a wife, they chose to distance themselves. Years later, in speaking with one of the Fitzsimmons cousins, I found that she remembers Pa Walsh with affection. However, her upbringing had been in Pa and Ma's home, for her parents lived upstairs on Depot Street, and her mother, my father's favorite sister, Alice, had married an Irishman, Francis Fitzsimmons.

Despite my grandparent's feelings, my mother and father were happy, but their life was not an easy one. On August 17, 1923, my brother, Paul was born, and ten days later, Mom suffered an embolus to the brain, causing aphasia and paralysis of her right side. She recovered her speech and motion, but the after effects of the stroke left her unable to use her right hand for dexterous activities. Having won a certificate for beautiful handwriting in high school, her letters after the stroke were typical of one who has learned to write in adulthood with the "wrong hand."

For a time, my parents lived with my Pop's sister, Agnes, but eventually they moved to 822 N. Main Street in Forest City, where three more children would be born: Aileen, on the same day as Paul in 1925, I, in 1931, and Florence, in 1935.

***

My first memory was from April 1935 when I was four-years-old. It was then that I saw Grandma Walsh lying in her coffin in the front living room at 66 Depot Street after she succumbed in a diabetic coma. Seven months later, on November 22, I was awakened by a commotion in Mom's bedroom. Tiptoeing inside, Mom said to me, "Go downstairs with Daddy." I did as I was told, and soon Nurse Lillian Hempstead Curtis appeared with a crying baby—my sister, Florence. I vividly recall my excitement at watching the nurse wiping Florence down and wrapping her in warm clothes.

America was in the grips of the depression at this time, and I particularly remember wearing a much hated brown and yellow gingham checked dress. One day, Mom surprised me with a brand-new red taffeta dress, which had a pleated collar and skirt and a black velvet belt. It was the most unforgettable dress—I felt like Shirley Temple—and so began my lifelong obsession with pretty clothes.

I don't know where Mom got the money for the new dress because employment was nearly unobtainable during the 1930's. The Chevrolet business which Pop's father owned and my dad operated, had failed in 1929, and as a result, Pop went to work for the Works Projects Administration. These were jobs designed by the Roosevelt administration to give a man a reason to get out of bed in the morning—building roads, highways, water and sewer lines and the like. Pop earned one dollar a day, and I would go to the Slovenian market and buy a chuck roast for fifty-nine cents a pound, a loaf of bread for eighteen cents, and a quart of milk for ten cents. A new Chevrolet vehicle sold for a whopping seven-hundred-eighty-five dollars in 1929!

At school, we were often given canned peaches and other surplus food, but the smell was objectionable to me, so I seldom ate them. Later in life, I would believe that growing up during the Great Depression had not greatly affected me, but I do recall the endless hunger, and longing to be anything but a 'beanpole," as I never weighed more than 115 pounds. I was taught to re-use, re-cycle, and conserve; for material possessions were few and far between.

We had no refrigerators then, only ice boxes which we used to keep items cold. These were two compartment oak boxes, one for ice and the other for food, with a pan below to collect the melted ice water which required daily emptying. Each day, the milkman, delivered a quart of milk to the doorstep, and if one didn't bring it in soon enough, the cream would freeze and push up the cardboard top of the glass bottle. In the summer, we children often followed the ice truck, which carried large blocks of ice cut from Ice Pond—now Kennedy Park. The Iceman chipped the blocks of ice to fit one's icebox on the rear of a flatbed trailer drawn by horses, and we children would snatch up the chips as a refreshing treat on those hot, broiling days!

We kept a steel box outside the kitchen window in winter, and this is where we stored meats and butter. Shopping was done almost daily, for the vagaries of the weather could not be trusted to keep meats frozen.

Our washing machine was a big tub with motor and wringer placed next to the bathtub, for the clothes had to be wrung out by inserting them into an attached wringer consisting of two rollers swung over the sink or tub. They were then placed in the bathtub to rinse, wrung again, and toted downstairs and outside to the energy-efficient line. Every Monday morning clothes could be seen flapping in the breeze, and housewives competed to have their laundry flying first, the earlier, the better. To this day, the smell of air-dried sheets reminds me of home!

We used Fels-Naptha soap and Rinso which unlike today's modern ones, were not very good detergents. I remember the white clothes being soaked in the bathtub in a Clorox solution on Sunday night for washday on Monday. Doing laundry consumed a whole day, and after drying starched shirts, and blouses made of cotton, these would be brought in, promptly dampened and ironed within an inch of their life! Perma-press and knit clothes did not come into fashion until the 1970s.

In winter, Mom persisted in hanging the clothes out to dry, but all they did was freeze, and so we took them off the line around 4:00 p.m. and re-hung them in the attic two floors up until they air-dried. Doing laundry was not for the faint of heart!

Until the 1960's, when she remarried and her husband, Joseph Novak, insisted that she buy an automatic washer and dryer, Mom hung on to the "old ways." In 1955, one of my treasures in our first new home was an automatic washer. The weekly schedule, (adhered to unless a holiday occurred on that day) was: washing on Monday, ironing on Tuesday, cleaning the upstairs on Thursday, the downstairs on Friday, and the kitchen on Saturday.

Spring housecleaning was a major project. Windows had to be washed on the second floor by removing them from their sashes to do the outside. Curtains and doilies were washed and starched, dresser drawers cleaned out, furniture washed and polished, and worst of all, carpets and pads dragged out of the house and draped over the line to be beaten with a wire handled beater. Afterward, they would be put back down on the floor, where they were scrubbed and vacuumed.

Pop and I hated spring housecleaning, but to Mom, it must have felt like a spiritual cleansing, for it was a ritual she continued until she was eighty-nine-years-old and went into the nursing home.

Although life could be challenging at that time, it was simpler too. Neighbors shared what little they had, and visiting each other was the usual Sunday occupation— most homes did not have phones until the 1950s.

Though we were poor, we did not feel deprived—everyone was in the same straits. Dad always made us feel good about ourselves. He didn't exhibit his Irish temper frequently. Instead, he prodded us to good behavior with, "Don't make Mom angry; do as you're told." One of his favorite expressions was, "It's no sin to be poor, but it's damned inconvenient."

***

One Sunday, when I was eight-years-old and attending the 10:30 high Mass, I became fascinated by the four-part harmony of the choir. I thought it was beautiful, and I made a decision to be a part of a group who made music. My music career, both solo and in choirs, began at St. Agnes Church, where I joined the choir and remained a member for over forty years. I also participated in the Forest City High School and Community Choruses, the Broome County Pops where I was a member for twenty years, and the Northeastern Philharmonic Chorus, in which I was able to sing operatic choruses. I often sang solo for funerals, weddings, and banquets as well.

Singing was a passion of mine that brought me out of my shell. As a child, I was very shy and withdrawn, sitting quietly and often biting my nails. However, in the ninth grade, I was chosen to sing a rendition of "White Christmas" at a High School assembly and loved every second of it. I loved the attention it attracted, and the fact that it also garnered me the soprano solo at the Susquehanna Chorus, in "Going Home."

Music has always played a great role in my family life. In fact, Mom had the leading role in her high school senior play and so did I. Performing onstage in the lead role of "A Date with Judy," when the first act began I threw myself onto a sectional sofa at the junction and as it separated, I fell to the floor. The audience thought it was part of the play, and that was when I discovered how much fun it was to make people laugh.

At home, I often sat at the piano and played for hours, during which Pop made me feel like a virtuoso. He always listened and never criticized. I loved playing for him, and I eagerly played the songs he loved. When Florence took lessons, the only number she seemed to play was "Fur Elise" but our dad listened as if she were a budding piano genius!

Pop, too, could frequently be heard singing "The Isle of Capri" and "My Wild Irish Rose" to my mother as he put on his cap and went out to the shed to get coal for the kitchen stove. The primary occupation I remember my father having while I was growing up was delivering wood and coal. I will always remember him sitting in the rocker in the kitchen, or on the back porch, for he went out early to make those deliveries. Mom, however, related that "he was often unemployed, and had eleven different jobs" during my youth. Perhaps, but I seldom recall Florence or myself being "home alone."

On Sunday, December 7, 1941, while walking into the William Stratford home after the Sunday matinee, an incident occurred that affected me deeply and still does. It was the announcement on the radio of the bombing of Pearl Harbor and President Roosevelt's words that it would be "A day that will live in infamy." As I walked home, everything seemed eerily quiet, and I wondered what effect the War would have on me.

My brother, Paul soon enlisted in the Navy, attending boot camp at Sampson, New York and training as a Pharmacist's Mate. This resulted in his transfer to the "Fleet Marines," and training at the Philadelphia Naval Hospital. On May 29, 1945, he was part of the landing forces on Okinawa, and in June, a telegram from the War Department arrived at our home. Though I was only thirteen, I knew this was serious and so I called Mom at Burns' Restaurant where she was employed. The telegram informed us that Paul was wounded while landing on Okinawa. He and two buddies were shot; he through the foot, and they, fatally.

Another incident from this time that is seared into my memory is the death of President Franklin Roosevelt in Warm Springs, Georgia, eighty-two days into his unprecedented fourth term. The beating of the drums at his solemn funeral procession impressed and saddened me, as did the films of crowds of sobbing people, both black and white, alongside the railroad tracks as his body was transported back to Washington, and then to Hyde Park, where he lies buried. The respect and love of the people he had served was so clearly expressed by the sadness and tears. He had been our only President in all my young life.

Paul spent four months recuperating at the Naval Hospital on

Guam, and, but for the wonder drug, penicillin, (newly discovered and utilized on many war wounds) would probably have lost his foot. This ended Paul's participation in the war, but I later found out that, as a medic, he carried no gun—only bandages! Are bullets selective because one wears a Red Cross on his arm, I wondered?

May 8, 1945, brought news of the end of the war with Germany. Though relieved, my family was still concerned, for Paul was stationed in the Pacific Theatre. On August 6, 1945, an atomic bomb was dropped on Hiroshima and on the 9th, another on Nagasaki, leaving over 140,000 people dead or maimed. The enormity of the power of destruction still leaves me dumbfounded. Undoubtedly, the decision to do so was not an easy one for President Truman and his cabinet, but they reasoned that by not doing so, more Americans would die. For our next step was to invade Japan.

It took another six days, but on August 15, 1945, while I scrubbed the kitchen floor and listened to the radio, the jubilant announcement was finally made. "The Japanese have surrendered." My brother would be coming home! Church bells pealed, and sirens sounded. People danced in the streets, and everyone gave a great sigh of relief that our young men would soon be home.

People gathered in the churches to pray and give thanks—to pray for those who would never come home and give thanks for those who would. Finally, the conflict was ended, and the rationing of flour, sugar, shortening and gas was over. During those years, a white lard-like substance named Oleo, which required one to pop a yellow capsule and mix it in, had been a butter substitute.

There was no joy, however, in the homes where a Gold Star hung in the front windows. Those gold star mothers were honored every year on Memorial Day as were their sons who had made the supreme sacrifice.

Paul witnessed the signing of the surrender by the Japanese Commander in China, (where he was later assigned before he came home) and wrote of the terrible anger of that leader. Japan, a nation with no natural resources, had attacked us at Pearl Harbor on December 7, 1941, while President Roosevelt was negotiating with the Japanese ambassador in Washington! Many years later, the Japanese Commander of the aircraft carrier from which the planes struck, stated, "I knew it was a losing battle from the start."

When Paul finally returned home from the war, he bought a big white horse whose name was "Pete." For the privilege of riding him whenever Paul was not, my brother conned me into caring for the animal by mucking out the barn, currying, shoveling manure and feeding "Pete." Many were the lazy afternoons and Sundays when "Pete" and I traversed the woods and valleys of Pennsylvania, enjoying every moment. Pop would often come out to the barn to talk with me while I did the chores, so I had an especially close relationship with my dad.

Fifty years after World War Two ended, I found a scrapbook I had made of the Pacific campaign, and around that same time, I also watched the "Landing on Okinawa" on the *History Channel*. I can only imagine the terror and horrors my brother must have experienced. He, like most veterans of that war, never talked about them, but he showed us his foot shortly before he died which clearly showed the trajectory scar of the bullet. We were all gathered at his house—me, my Mom, my sisters, Florence and Aileen, Aileen's husband, Russ, Paul and his wife, Ellen—when the talk drifted to the war, and Paul and Russ' participation in it. Russ had been on a transport ship and came through unscathed, but Paul took off his shoe and, for the first time, told about his wounding. He also suffered from a fungal infection of his hands and feet, which he referred to as "jungle rot." Paul died shortly after this gathering on January 4, 1989.

CHAPTER TWO

The war ended the Depression, and prosperity began to come over America. Cars were advertised and sold by the millions—the war had stopped the production of cars, and all factories had been ordered to produce tanks, planes, and jeeps. We had gotten a new car in 1942, on the eve of Florence's birthday. Pa Walsh had had a heart attack, so Pop's sister, Mary had inherited his Buick and in turn, we inherited her car: a 1936 Chevrolet.

For over twenty years, it was the only model we ever owned, and it took us on many a Sunday drive over the farmland in Pennsylvania. Most notably, down a steep hill to the Barriger farm near Pleasant Mount. Bessie and Jim Barriger were old, even then, but they still milked cows and canned vegetables, and Pop loved visiting them. One night while at their farm, and after poring over the Sears catalog and picking out our Easter outfits, my younger sister, Florence and I became hungry. Noticing some "stew" on the kitchen stove, we decided to help ourselves. After supper, Bessie picked up the kettle and said "Guess I better feed ole Shep." Shep was the dog, and grossed out, Florence and I looked at each other and gagged! Bessie always threw the scraps into that pot and fed the dog with them at the end of the day. Needless to say, we never did that again!

***

The war had wrought changes in my family, but as a child, I didn't notice them so much. We still entertained ourselves by gathering around the radio, where the Lone Ranger prompted me to be a "Girl of the West" in my dreams, and the Texaco broadcast of the Saturday afternoon opera stimulated perceptions that I, too, could be an opera star. To this day, the "Grand Ole Opry" gives me comfort, for Pop always listened to it on Saturday night as I went to sleep. Days were spent in reading, sewing, mowing the lawn, helping with housework and laundry, and especially, playing the piano—again, envisioning my becoming a national virtuoso. We always looked forward to Saturday and Sunday when a movie could be seen for only twenty-five cents. Some of the best movies of that era were biographies of Chopin and Gershwin; I came home inspired to become a famous pianist!

School was always one of my favorite things, and I was extremely active in extracurricular activities. In addition to playing the piano and acting in the school plays, I was also an honor student, cheerleader, avid dancer and reader. When I completed the Home Economics course, newly inserted in the high school curriculum for females, I became an active sewer as well. Using an old treadle Singer sewing machine Mom possessed, I developed a lifelong love for sewing.

As active as I was, I had no time and no desire for getting into trouble. We looked forward to the Friday night basketball games and the friendly rivalry with Vandling, which had extremely good teams for the size of their school. I also enjoyed dances and going to the movies on Saturday and Sunday afternoons.

On January 2, 1945, an event occurred that shook the small

town of Forest City, to its very core. A nine-year-old girl, Mae Barrett, was found brutally murdered, her body hidden in an abandoned house in Vandling.

Much to my horror, one week later, a young schoolboy, thirteen-year-old Myron Semunchick was arrested for the crime. I was stunned, and shocked beyond belief. I knew Myron; up until a few days ago I considered him a friend. In fact, only the weekend before Mae's murder, I had sat with Myron at the movie theatre on Saturday, and on Sunday, he and another boy, Louis Jerin had walked me home!

When Pop discovered that I had sat at the Saturday matinee with the thirteen-year-old murderer, he reined us in with an iron hand. Little did I know that this was not the only experience I would have with a murderer! Murder, especially in small towns like Forest City and Vandling, was an unknown entity, (only two were committed in the past century), and so families maintained a closer watch on their children, and doors which had never been locked before were now bolted shut.

When the 9:00 o'clock whistle blew, (the curfew which had been enacted in 1916 to keep children under 16 off the streets), it was time to be off the streets. Children were seen rushing home before the siren completed its cycle. Parents monitored their children's every movement, and so I rarely gave my parents problems with disobedience.

I do remember the first time I tried alcohol. I was seventeen, and after attending a prom, my date told me to "chug-a-lug" a glass of wine and I did. I didn't like the way the alcohol left me feeling "out of control" and so I never took more than two drinks at any function I ever attended.

I graduated from high-school in 1948, and was honored to give the graduation speech, which was titled, "The Fiftieth Graduating class of Forest City High School." I wasn't sure what I wanted to do with my life. I had often sat in the gym—also used as a study hall—at the old Forest City High School and pondered what my future held. Mom had forced me to take two years of stenography and typing, but I also took academic courses, anticipating something more for my future than being a secretary. Hanging on the gym wall was a poster of a proud nurse with a white cap and red cape flung over her shoulder, her eyes looking into the great beyond. That poster inspired me. In March of 1948, I asked my brother, Paul for five dollars to go to St. Joseph's Hospital School of Nursing in Carbondale to take the entrance exam, but I didn't tell Mom.

Paul seemed amused, and hooted, "You can't even stand the sight of blood! You're going to be a nurse?"

I took the bus to Carbondale anyway, walked up the hill to the hospital, and took the exam. The only question on the test I remember was, "Why do you want to be a nurse?" Apparently, they liked my answer, for I was accepted into St. Joseph's Hospital School of Nursing.

When the letter of acceptance arrived, Mom was wringing

clothes and was so shocked she nearly put her arm through the wringer. She had never known me to express a desire to "be something."

The admission fee was two hundred and fifty dollars which included books, uniforms, and scissors, which no nurse should be without. It was an astronomical amount of money in the late 1940's, and Mom and Pop were not wealthy, but Pop had just begun a new business, F.P. Walsh and Son Company. It was around this time that people began converting from coal to fuel oil, and Pop bought a tanker truck and started the company with my brother, Paul. Still, the average weekly income was less than eighty dollars and Pop's health was slowly deteriorating. Somehow, my parents managed to come up with the money, so on a hot August day, I found myself sitting in a dorm room with three other girls, all of us excited to begin our new careers.

I never lived at home again except on my days off during nurses' training. Sometimes on those days off I would accompany Pop on his fuel deliveries, driving the tanker to the outlying farms and thinking I was a "cool dude" up there in the cab, double-clutching that truck over the hills of Pennsylvania! Mom continued to operate the fuel oil business after Pop's death but eventually sold it to my brother-in-law, John Kowalewski, who changed the name to K.W. Oil Company. The business still exists and is currently operated by John's two sons, John and David.

That humid day in August, however, marked my

indoctrination into another world that would occupy over forty-five years of my life. I remember well the day my Mom and I arrived for my three-year stay in an old convent, formerly used by the Immaculate Heart of Mary nuns. There were four girls to a dorm, each of us with a small desk and chair, twin bed, half of a dresser and a locker. Bringing clothes to travel home did not involve many outfits. We were furnished with maxi skirted starched uniforms, scissors, and a woolen cape—navy with a red lining— and informed to bring: cotton slips, white nylon hose, regulation two-inch heeled nurses' rubber soled shoes, pajamas, housecoats, slippers, bras, and girdles. Proper undergarments were even necessary for me; a one-hundred-fifteen-pound lean girl!

Meeting my roommates, Kay, Rosemary, and Rosemarie was a new experience. Kay became my best friend, but Rosemarie was an only child who did not mesh well with the others in the room. I later was told her father was a member of the Mafia, and she had no friends, so living with her was a challenge.

From the first day we entered the hospital, we were taught Nursing Arts, which mainly consisted of housekeeping your patients' surroundings. Since we had a male who mopped the floors, we became responsible for the cleanliness of our patient's bed area—cleaning the bedside stand, changing the water in the flowers, and making the patient comfortable. Daily, we were assigned a number of patients who had to be bathed, given the bedpan and fed if they were unable to eat on their own. Patients were hospitalized for greater lengths of time then. A stroke patient might stay for months, new mothers, ten days, and operative patients did not get out of bed for at least two days. Many fractured hip patients lived and died in those beds, months after admittance. Bed rest was advised for everyone who was admitted, especially heart attack patients.

At 10:00 a.m. we began classes where, over the next three years, we took courses in anatomy, physiology, chemistry, obstetrics, pharmaceuticals, and psychiatry. After lunch, we would return to the classroom for another two hours. In our first year, after a meager supper which often consisted of macaroni salad and spiced ham, we returned to the floor to prepare the patients for sleep. This entailed rubbing their backs and changing the draw sheet, a short sheet with which we moved them. After giving the night medications, visitors were asked to leave, and the lights turned out. Excessive noise was not allowed, and only small night lights along the floor were lit.

After the first three months, I was assigned to the evening shift, where I saw my first patient die. Helping a senior nurse give evening care, she asked me to help turn a patient on his side so she could wash his back. I knew the man looked and breathed differently from my other patients and required a full bed-bath. He was dying of kidney failure and had what was known as "nephritic frost" over his body. As I held him, he gurgled and stopped breathing.

I had never seen a person die before and immediately began to cry, wondering if this was really what I wanted to do for the rest of my life. The nurse said to me, "It's okay. We have to wash him anyway." I was seventeen-years-old, and not prepared for this, but somehow we "completed the care of the dead."

My brother's wife, Ellen was expecting a child, and one night while I was in supervised study from 7:00 p.m. to 9:00 p.m. I saw Paul outside in the maternity waiting room. I was so excited about the impending birth of my niece that I asked Sister if I could accompany Ellen into the labor room. No one was allowed in the delivery room in 1948, but the Doctor took pity on me and told me to stand in the corner and "Don't touch anything." As the baby's head was emerging, the doctor glanced up and later told me that he thought my eyes were going to pop out of my head. I'll admit, I was shocked. I thought babies came out feet first, but this big bulging turned out to be my niece's head. Forty-five years later, I was privileged to be with my daughter at Medical College of Georgia when she delivered her fourth baby, and it is still the most exciting thing I've ever observed.

From morning to night, every minute of our day was programmed for us. We were awakened for breakfast and then expected to attend daily Mass at 6:30; then it was floor duty, classes, lunch, more classes, supper and more studying. Lights out was 10:00 p.m. We were rarely out of the hospital, and when we were, we were expected to be in full uniform. We represented a profession and were expected to dress and behave accordingly. No shorts or tank tops were allowed in the cafeteria.

Initially, we had weekends off, but after six months, and receiving our "cap," we were required to work nights and weekends. Being a day person, that was almost my downfall! Two of us were assigned an entire floor of up to forty-two patients, and responsible for performing many tasks—administering medication, changing oxygen tanks, admitting new patients, and charting all the activities of the night. Our mornings began by giving wash basins to patients who could clean themselves up, and bedpans to those who couldn't use the bathroom. We also prepared the Catholic patients for daily communion, which Father administered at 6:00 a.m. Ironically, the Sisters would often comment that they never saw us out walking, or getting any exercise—we didn't have any free time, and when we did, all we longed for was a nap!

The nuns were well aware that we were young females, and if we became friendly with any of the servicemen who were so prevalent at the time, we were promptly assigned night duty—as though we couldn't do in the day what was more often done at night! The nuns were good to us, however, throwing Halloween and Christmas parties that were both memorable and fun. One Halloween, having been on the cleanup committee, I was delayed getting back to the dorm, and when I finally crawled into bed, I felt a cold, wet "snake" slither up my leg. Leaping out of bed and screaming, I soon discovered that one of my roommates had put a cold hot dog between my sheets! Short sheeting was often done, and frequently a girdle was found hanging from the light switch by its garter. The nuns, although they tried, were hard pressed to quell us lively girls.

By our second year of nursing school, we were no longer "probies," and were now allowed to give meds without supervision. We knew how to change a bandage, and were expert at hospital bed making and bedpan administration, but there was a lot of hard work that nurses today are not required to do. For instance, we often went off duty moaning with raw hands, for before we threw dirty or bloody sheets down the laundry, we had to pre-wash them. Oh, how we prayed for someone to discover an adult diaper or a hole in the mattress for our incontinent patients! But we cared about our work and truly believed we were making a difference.

That same year we traveled to Scranton for our pediatric affiliation and then to Baltimore for psychiatry. For some of the girls, it was the first time they had ever traveled outside of the area. In Baltimore, the nuns held a mixer for us and invited the young Air Corpsmen from nearby Fort Meade which made for a lovely and enjoyable evening, but I had already met someone on my trip down. When the five of us girls boarded the Greyhound bus in Scranton, three Navy men also got on and decided to sit behind us. Before we got to Bloomsburg, two of the men had introduced themselves. One of them, Stanley (Stan) Coar seemed interested in me and his friend, Vic, seemed to have his eye on my classmate, Kay. Little did I know that this was a propitious meeting.

Stan Coar was handsome and fun to be with, and he and Vic

came to Baltimore every other weekend. Soon we were seeing each other exclusively. Stan was adventurous too. One day, he and Vic had been flying back to Norfolk, Virginia after a weekend in Scranton when their two-seater Army surplus plane crashed into a chicken coop in Daleville. They were flying illegally, as they had a third passenger sitting on Stan's lap. They also had no landing lights and no clearance, and they were about to be AWOL, as they were supposed to be back at base by 8:00 a.m. and it was already 3:00 when they crashed.

The farmer, into whose chicken coop they crashed, came running out of his house brandishing a rifle, sure that the ruckus was a fox in the hen-house. Instead, he found three men and a crashed plane! I think Stan was more scared of that gun than the crash itself.

By Christmas, Stan was already talking marriage, but I stalled him—he made the service sound so exciting that I, too, considered joining the Navy and "seeing the world." Instead, I ended up planning our August 21, 1951, wedding!

Baltimore was my first introduction to a big city, and I loved it. Needless to say, psychiatry was not my favorite subject; I didn't want to be stuck inside studying, I wanted to be out on the town. When January rolled around, and we were scheduled to return to Carbondale, none of us wanted to go. There was so much to see and do in Baltimore, while Carbondale was dull, drab and boring in comparison. Even worse, because I now had a beau, I was promptly put on nights in the nursery where I took care of as many as forty babies.

One incident I will never forget was the labor and delivery of an Italian woman laboring with her twelfth child. Being poor, she'd had no prenatal care, and as she sat looking out the window of the labor room, she said to me, "I lost my sixth baby in this hospital and this time, you are going to lose me." My years of nursing have taught me that people often have an omen of their deaths which I've learned to respect. Returning from dinner at 5:00 p.m. I walked into the delivery room and saw the Italian woman lying dead on the table, a beautiful twelve-pound baby boy screaming in the background. Our OB-GYN supervisor sat outside, her head in her hands—for forty years she'd assisted mothers and their babies and this death really affected her, as it did all of us. Looking back, I think the Italian woman probably had an amniotic fluid embolism, and nothing is more dramatic, for it happens so suddenly that no one can do a thing about it.

The operating room was another assignment which I was partial to—never dreaming I would spend thirty years of my life in the OR. The age of specialization had not yet begun, and nurses were trained to give good bedside nursing. For fifteen years I did private duty nursing, simply for the convenience of not being tied to a regular schedule.

Looking back, I realize that they were the best years of my life. In the daily dramas that occurred, no two days were ever the same. I worked harder than I thought possible, learned discipline that forever established what I would become and relished the episodes of life and death I'd been privy to. What I treasured most of all, however, were the friendships that were forged.

Those three years of nursing school flew by; marked by maturity, understanding, and kindness for a fellow suffering creature. I especially loved surgery and obstetrics and enjoyed studying patient charts, trying to diagnose illnesses based on the lab work, symptoms, and findings. In another time, if females had been more freely accepted into medical school, and costs were not beyond my parents' means, I'd have gladly gone to medical school, but that was not to be.

One of the most memorable experiences from that time was graduation day, and my father, whose health was rapidly deteriorating, getting out of his sickbed to stand proudly with tears in his eyes as we proceeded down the aisle and onto the stage. I was the first one in his family to go on to higher education, and he was proud.

CHAPTER THREE

Pop's health had begun to decline when I was still in nursing school. One night in 1950, coming home from a date, I noticed that the house was lit up like a Christmas tree. Rushing inside, I found to my horror, Pop's spittoon bucket filled with blood—the result of a lung hemorrhage. Being in nurses' training, I began studying lung conditions and suspected that my Pop was suffering from tuberculosis. If so, I knew his days were numbered, for at that time there were no drugs with which to treat it. Dr. MacAndrew encouraged me to give him injections of Streptomycin, a newly discovered drug used on servicemen to prevent infection, but untried on tuberculosis.

"What do we have to lose, Anne," the doctor said gently, "He has a fatal disease."

He was right, of course, but Pop had so little body fat that it was difficult to find a spot for the intramuscular injections. Streptomycin, in an oil base, necessitated the use of a large bore needle. Streptomycin was one of the "miracle drugs" which gave him a few more years. Later, a combination of Isoniazid. PAS and Rifampin were found to cure the disease, one of the great discoveries of the twenty-first century.

***

Stan and I were married on August 21, 1951, and one of the first pieces of furniture we purchased was a combination hi-fidelity radio and record player. We both loved the same kinds of music—

country and western, Broadway show tunes and the current radio favorites—and soon, we began an extensive collection of records and tapes. While I sang in the church choir, Stan often composed his own music.

We were living in Norfolk, Virginia as Stan was still in the Navy, and it was there that we welcomed our first child, Anne on March 23, 1952. Anne was a beautiful baby, brash, assertive, and a joy to raise. In 1953 our second child, Cathy was born. She and Anne were like Irish twins and grew to be extremely close.

Not long after Cathy's birth, Mom called us to come home, saying, "Daddy is dying." When we arrived, Pop's bed was out in the back yard and fearing that we were too late, I became hysterical and was hardly able to get out of the car. As we opened the door, however, there was Pop in a new bed in the living room, and I was so relieved! He had accidentally overdosed on Demerol, for with long days confined to bed, the time passed slowly. Mom worked at the Endicott Johnson Shoe Factory, located in Forest City behind our house, and Florence was in school. Pop often took large doses of medication, which he never measured. He would take the bottle of Agarol, for instance, and guzzle a swig. He recovered from this episode, but died a year later, on April 1, 1954.

We were back in Norfolk by then, and I was due to give birth to our third child so was unable to return home to Pennsylvania for Pop's funeral. Two weeks after he passed away, our third child and first son, Larry was born.

I enjoyed living in Norfolk. I was elected President of the Bromley Garden Club, sang in the church choir, and loved being a part of a growing young population which made for some memorable times. The weather was temperate—snow falling only one day in the ten years we resided there—and the springtime was absolutely breathtaking, with all the blooming daffodils, azaleas, dogwoods, and rhododendrons which grew among the evergreens. The Navy wives got together for monthly luncheons, when we'd hoe out our homes, prepare a main dish and entertain. Baby showers were a frequent occurrence as well, for we were just beginning our families.

Stan had mustered out of the Navy in January 1954, and we made the decision to stay in Virginia. A building boom was occurring in Norfolk. The Korean War had ended, but the "Cold War" had begun, and so the need for housing escalated. Norfolk was the largest Navy base on the East coast, and every acre of ground and farmland was sold for development.

Since I worked private duty—ICUs were unheard of at that time—we needed two cars. Stan became a salesman, and his income was sporadic. The sales jobs were paid by commission only, but he usually made at least fifty-dollars a week. The only real constant was my income—and my pregnancies. After Larry, Mike arrived in 1955 and Aileen in 1957.

They were happy years. Friends dropped in to share a meal, and we often had guests for holidays since we were financially unable to travel home to Pennsylvania more than once a year.

We'd host Halloween and New Year's Eve parties when we'd roll up the area rug in the dining room, borrow chairs for seating, and dance until the wee hours. Stan was selling the Americana Encyclopedia at the time and his boss, Worth Pittman, often had Saturday night poker parties. There were many Saturdays when the other salesmen, in particular Bill Wendell, would accompany Stan home and we'd have coffee and watch the "Tonight" show.

There were also bowling nights and dinners honoring the top salesmen, and often we would go to the Navy Chief's Club; the only place drinking was allowed, as Norfolk was a "dry town" at the time. Illegal liquor—called "White Lightening"—was obtainable at a nearby still and it truly lived up to its name. It was powerful! We made new friends every year as the sailors' tour of duty seldom spanned more than two years, and several of those people have remained our friends for more than fifty years. Namely, Albert and Margaret Wagner, and Byron and Elaine Buley.

As the children came into our lives, their care occupied all our time and stamina. We had moved four times in three years, and Stan changed jobs often. He was a hard worker, who never went a day without employment in the thirty years of our marriage.

Our growing family had outgrown our two bedroom apartment on Baffin Road and, wanting a place of our own, we began visiting "open houses" every Sunday. Eventually, we found a Cape Cod, Levitt-built house with four bedrooms and two baths at 1801

Tulane Road. We moved in seven days after Michael's birth, on October 17, 1955, and thank goodness for Elaine Buley, who went over to the new house and made beds, unwrapped dishes, and put away groceries while I stayed behind to watch her two children and my four. The house cost $11,000 and Stan, eligible for a G.I loan put twenty-five-dollars down.

While Stan and his friends were trucking our possessions over to the new house and unloading the last of the furniture, someone stole our mattress, leaving us to sleep on our box spring for a few months.

It was an exciting, but stressful time. The daily care of four, and then five children was eased by the fact that there were at least thirty children in the neighborhood. Like most families who acquire a home, a station wagon, a swing set, a picnic table and a sand box in the backyard, we had also acquired debt. Although credit cards were unheard of, we were paying a mortgage and owed on furniture purchased when Stan left the Navy.

During this time, I accepted a part-time job in the office of Dr. J. DiCiero, an oral surgeon. One day, the doctor told me to, "Get behind the dental chair" and as he gave the patient the Sodium Brevital, to anesthetize him, I continued the nitrous oxide and oxygen administration by nasal mask. Afterward, I told the doctor, "This is what I want to be when I grow up!" However, after investigating attending anesthesia school at Norfolk General, I learned that it involved being single, available to be on call, and an erratic class schedule geared toward the operating room, as the students were utilized to practice on the patients. Definitely too much for a young mother to take on.

***

In 1961, Stan decided we should return to Pennsylvania, and although I was reluctant to leave Norfolk, I finally agreed. That October, we bought a beautiful home at 407 Main Street in the small town of Vandling, which we would occupy for the next twenty-one years.

Initially, I was sorry we returned home, for employment was not easy to obtain and we had two mortgages to pay; one in Virginia and now the one here. Stan was still working on commission, and with only one car, it was a struggle.

Eventually, we sold the Virginia house and Stan began working for the Americana Corporation collecting on delinquent accounts in Florida and Georgia. He worked seven days a week, for three weeks at a time, and then flew home to spend a week with the family. It was a salaried position with an expense account, and having a weekly income was marvelous. Raising five children alone was not.

Stan usually flew back and forth to Florida, leaving his car at the airport, and bought me a 1954 Oldsmobile to use at home. One afternoon we used my car to drive to the airport and Stan unloaded his luggage, then put the car keys in his pocket and boarded the plane. Too late, I realized that he'd taken my keys with him. I informed the attendant at the terminal, and another plane flying back from Newark brought me the keys. By the time I got home to Vandling that night, Stan was already in Florida.

In early 1963, I discovered that I was pregnant again. Stan was still with the Americana Corporation, but one night he returned home unexpectedly and crawled into bed beside me.

"What are you doing home?" I asked, surprised.

He hesitated for a moment before saying, "The firm was bought out by another. They eliminated my job, so I drove home from Florida."

Although Stan never complained about not having a college education, I think it bothered him. His father had wanted him to attend the Naval Academy or West Point, but he had failed the physical because he wore glasses. When he learned that his brother, Larry had obtained a job in the Empire State Building, Stan remarked, "That's what a college education will do for one."

Stanley Jr. or "Curly Chop," as his father called him—later to be amended simply to "Chopper"—was born in August of 1963, at St. Joseph's Hospital where I had done my nurse's training.

Stan took various sales jobs, the last of which was at Fairview Memorial Park selling cemetery plots. I never understood why someone would buy a plot before they needed it!

In December 1964, one year after Chopper's birth I met Olga, an alumna of St. Joseph's, at a Christmas party. Olga was working at Moses Taylor Hospital in Scranton, and, having never forgotten my job with Dr. DeCeiro, I asked her how I could get into an anesthesia school.

"Apply," Olga answered with a grin.

Since returning to Pennsylvania in 1961, I had held only sporadic jobs—mostly private duty nursing. Thinking about becoming a nurse anesthetist made me realize that I needed a definite income, and so I applied to Wayne Memorial Hospital. After a nine-month stint on medical, surgical and obstetrical floors—and having worked all the holidays in the interim—I decided to apply as Olga had suggested. In October 1965 I was accepted at Moses Taylor Hospital School of Anesthesia, the only student of Dr. Ernest Shandor.

If I thought nursing school was difficult, it was nothing compared to anesthesia school. My typical day began at 4:00 a.m.—quiet time to study—then waking the children, getting them ready for school and dressing Chopper to go to the baby-sitters. Afterward, I would drive the twenty-five miles to Scranton, where I worked in both the operating room and doing clinical experience before having class time in the afternoon. Leaving the hospital around 4:00 p.m. I would arrive home to do laundry, prepare dinner, clean up, and play with Chopper. I could not have done it without help from my older children, each of whom had their assigned duties.

Once a week I shopped for groceries, and then stopped at Montdale Dairy Farm, where I discovered I could buy seven gallons of milk more cheaply than at the supermarket. (Seven gallons, that's what the children drank each week!) Sometimes as a treat, I'd also stop at Kentucky Fried Chicken for our dinner, and arrive home at six or seven o'clock. Looking back, I marvel that I was able to do this.

At the time, anesthesia consisted of the administration of open-drop ether, whereby a gauze mask was applied to the patient's face, and drops of ether dropped on it. This was a fairly safe and easy anesthetic, allowing one to monitor the patient's breathing and pupillary dilatation, as well as ascertain the depth of anesthesia. Its main hazards were that it was highly explosive, required a lengthy induction, and had a long recuperation with nausea and vomiting. Because "scavenging" the fumes—properly venting them outside the operating room—was not done until the Occupational Safety Administration decreed it in the 1970s, I was always exhausted, never realizing that as I administered the ether, I was drugging myself in the process.

Of course, new developments have been made since I poured open drop ether—halogenated inhalation agents such as Fluothane, Ethrane, and Penthrane were used in conjunction with nitrous oxide and oxygen. And as ambulatory surgery became more prominent, IV sedation with local anesthesia was more often used for such surgeries as hand and eye operations, spinal anesthesia for knee and hip operations and epidural for child deliveries became very prevalent. The most wonderful development was of Diprivan, because of its short action and the patient's ability to recover from it as soon as it was turned off. It also had few side effects like earlier anesthesia. (Michael Jackson was put to sleep permanently, with this drug.) It is also used for head injuries, allowing patients to recover from swelling of the brain and resistance to the respirator Diprivan can induce coma, which allows our servicemen and women, suffering from head injuries in Iraq and Afghanistan to be transported to trauma centers closer to home in fully equipped intensive care flights from the battlefield. The use of pulse oximeters has made anesthesia safer, for it's an immediate indication of oxygen deprivation.

Anesthesia school was an eighteen-month course, and I was paid the princely sum of fifty dollars a month, with fifty dollar increments every three months. During that entire time, I was allotted only two weeks of vacation. I found it a challenging occupation, with many emotional highs and lows. For instance, the second day in the school, I successfully intubated a patient and felt like it had been a breeze. Later, in class, when I learned all the hazards of intubation, like tubing the esophagus and thereby depriving the patient of oxygen, or rupturing the trachea, I developed "performance anxiety." It didn't last long, but it was there.

One of the greatest compliments ever paid to me was by a newly hired young anesthesiologist at Susquehanna Anesthesia who stated, "You know, Annie; there's only one person more skilled at intubation here than you."

"Who?" I asked innocently

"Me," he quipped, grinning.

The lows of the occupation were the night calls and the many patients who were diagnosed with cancer after the incision was made.

After eighteen months of schooling, and with no fanfare, I graduated and was handed my diploma in April 1967. I traveled to New York to take the National Anesthesia test and afterward while lunching with much younger students and comparing answers from the test I was horrified to realize that many of my answers didn't correspond with theirs. I departed New York despondent and convinced I had failed. Therefore, I was ecstatic when I received the news in July that I was now a certified registered nurse anesthetist; the beginning of a thirty-year career in my chosen field had begun.

I applied for work at Carbondale General Hospital, but they believed $10,000 was too much to pay in salary, so I took employment in an oral surgeon's office. The doctor was a "workaholic" who employed two nurse anesthetists. The hours were long, and the work constant—even requiring us to change bloody gauzes in patients' mouths while eating lunch. When the doctor told me he wanted me to work the 10:00 a.m. to 7:00 p.m. shift, I finally told him "good-bye." Such hours were simply unacceptable for a mother of six—I needed to see my family at some time!

After that, I decided to take a respite from working. Stan had applied for and obtained a job at IBM in Endicott, New York, and now that he had steady employment and was able to work overtime, I could sit back and just be a housewife. Stan would drive the one-hundred-thirty mile round-trip daily for the next sixteen years and eventually rise in the company to the level of quality control inspector.

***

I had long been intimidated by Stan's mother, who I thought of as a domineering woman, and she was one of the reasons I was leery of moving back to Pennsylvania. Getting to know her better, I soon realized my fears were unfounded. "Nana," as she was called, was a widow who was not only elegant, extremely polite, and diplomatic, but one who never interfered in our lives. She taught me a lot by her example. Nana owned a cottage on nearby Crystal Lake and often let Stan and me and the children use it. After her death from diabetic kidney failure on January 19, 1967, Stan bought a motorboat and taught the children how to water ski. We all spent many happy hours at the lake with them.

In addition to the boat, Stan also purchased two snowmobiles, and we enjoyed many winter hours in the clear, cold starlit nights traveling the country on them. Sometimes we'd even go as far as Old Forge, or New York, and soon we had joined a newly formed Snowmobile Club. The snowmobiles were not only used for enjoyment but sometimes to get to the hospital for emergencies when there were no other means of transportation.

It was probably a good thing that I had decided to take some time off of work because in 1968, I discovered that I was pregnant once again. During a cold and icy February night in 1969, our fourth daughter, Marilyn was born at Mercy Hospital. We brought her home in our newly acquired 1969 Ford station wagon—the only new car Stan and I would ever own—which could properly seat our ever-growing family. (At one point, Stan considered buying a used hearse, but I actively refused to be seen in one until my demise!)

CHAPTER FOUR

Things were changing. While I was at home with a new baby and a toddler, my oldest children were quickly growing up. In January 1970 an opportunity to teach part-time at the St. Joseph's School of Nursing arose, and I was forced to make a decision. Knowing that the four oldest children would soon be going off to college or getting married, and that we would need more income, I decided to accept the teaching position. Before long, the teaching included giving anesthesia and then worked its way into a full-time position; one for which I would have to be on call.

Our oldest daughter, Anne was planning to marry Stanley Kalasinski in January of 1971 and in October 1970, our second oldest daughter, Cathy became engaged to Todd Green. Although Todd was older than Cathy, we cheered her decision to marry him. He was a fine man—the son of our best friends—whom we liked very much. We knew he would make a good husband for our daughter.

Now, in addition to the new job and the new baby, plans for two weddings would have to be made. Additionally, around this same time, I discovered that I was pregnant yet again. 1971 would be a year like no other. In January, Anne and Stanley married. In May, Chopper made his First Holy Communion. On May 30, Stan and I bought our get-away cottage at Lewis Lake, and only days later; Cathy graduated from high school; my favorite aunt passed away; and our eighth and last child, Nancy was born—all of it occurring on the same day!

I was laid up for a while, having had to undergo a caesarean section with Nancy and a hysterectomy at the same time. Needless to say, those were the most stressful years of mine and Stan's marriage. Between trying to move necessities into our new cottage, two infants still in diapers—which amounted to daily washing of seven loads of laundry—battles over the car, teens with raging hormones, planning for Cathy's wedding and other issues, our home soon became a war zone. Sleepless nights didn't help, and our marriage was strained to the nth degree. At times, days would go by without us speaking for fear of disagreement, and there was no time to sit down and discuss our problems. It retrospect, I believe this was the most disastrous period of our marriage. The pressure became too much to handle, and I began to want out.

Adding to this stress, I discovered Stan's drinking had escalated from parties to every day. I had no clue about this until the babysitter informed me that she saw Stan's car at a local bar every morning. Each Saturday, Stan would drink all afternoon, come home happy, and soon pass-out on the couch. Throughout the 1970s, we attended few parties or dances—only family graduations or weddings—because Stan never stopped drinking once he began. He would drink until he passed-out, and whenever we did attend social functions, he would stand at the bar all night getting drunk. When I saw he could hardly navigate, I would plead a headache, and we'd leave which was always a harrowing experience in itself. Stan always insisted on driving which terrified me. He often put the car in reverse at stop signs and weaved all over the road. Sometimes he'd vomit as he staggered up the stairs to bed.

In 1976, Cathy and Todd held a beautiful Open House with family and friends for mine and Stan's twenty-fifth wedding anniversary. There was plenty of singing—three of the neighbors came down the driveway playing "When your old wedding ring was new," on their kazoos—and visiting with the guests, as well as wonderful food prepared by Cathy and her mother-in-law. It was a beautiful day, marred only by Stan's drunkenness. We arrived home at 5:00 p.m. and Stan was so drunk that he immediately passed-out. When his brother, Larry called to wish us a "Happy Anniversary" Stan was too drunk to even talk.

The Valentine's Day dance at the Legion Hall in 1977 was just about our last appearance in public. Stan got drunk, and around 10:30 p.m. simply disappeared. Arriving home to find he was not there, I searched the streets of Forest City, Vandling, and Browndale, looking for his fallen body in the snow. At 3:30 a.m., the babysitter finally called me on the CB and told me he was home. Where he had gone, and with whom, I never found out, but I was so angry, I decided never to attend another party with him.

I began attending Al-Anon meetings and realized that alcoholism is a disease. By then, however, our relationship was so strained that we rarely spoke to each other, except in regards to the children's schedules. In retrospect, we were a very dysfunctional family. Stan was a closet drinker—few people knew about it—and I was an enabler.

We attended our last social function together in 1978; a twenty-fifth wedding anniversary party for good friends at St. Basil's Hall in Simpson. Stan had a few vodka martinis before dinner, so when we sat down to eat, he was well on the way to getting drunk. As I watched him standing at the bar with another woman, laughing and talking and getting drunker by the minute, I became infuriated. Pleading a headache, I finally convinced him to leave, and as he could barely walk, this time, I drove. It was a warm evening, and Chopper was sitting at the kitchen table when we arrived home.

I was angry, and began thinking that it wasn't fair that I had to miss all the fun because my husband was a drunk, so I told Stan that I was returning to the party without him. Stan went ballistic and started choking me—thank goodness Chopper was there as he had to pull Stan off. Scared, I retreated into the bathroom and locked the door while Stan pleaded for me to come out and talk. I slept on the couch that night and vowed that I would be at the lawyer's office on Monday morning to begin divorce proceedings.

The next morning Stan came downstairs acting contrite. He tried to apologize and hug me, but I would have none of it. I told him I would be seeking the services of a lawyer on Monday, and he should prepare to move out. There would be no more attempts on my life while he was in his drunken rages and no chance that my children would be orphaned while he went to prison.

Coldly and calmly, I recited all the incidents of embarrassment, abuse, and hatred he'd heaped on me in his alcoholic rages. Stan sat at the kitchen table smoking one cigarette after another and drinking endless cups of coffee until he finally agreed to consult the AA organization. We drove to Scranton that very night to attend a meeting, and I finally realized that I was not alone. The horror stories I heard from others—of driving through garages, hitting poles and time spent in jail—matched mine. I prayed that this would be a new beginning for us; for our marriage and for Stan's sobriety. Only later did I learn that Stan's attack on me had nothing to do with his willingness to get help. His mentor told me that Stan had driven home from Endicott drunk the day before and remembered nothing of it and it scared him. To his credit, however, Stan never touched another drink. Not even when he went through the most devastating experience a human being could go through and everyone would have understood if he had.

***

The emotional highs and lows of the 1970's were extreme. That decade included six graduations, two weddings (in one year), two new babies, and two new grandchildren.

After two years of marriage, our daughter, Anne's marriage was on shaky ground. Although she and Stan Kalasinski had had a daughter together, Amy, the couple argued continuously and divorced in 1973.

In 1975, our son, Larry's girlfriend was tragically killed on his motorcycle. He graduated from the University of Pennsylvania Magna Cum Laude the following year, but it was a solemn time. Heartbroken that his girl was not there to share his joy, Larry threw himself into work and tried to get on with his life.

In 1976, Anne married again, this time to a young man named Michael Revak. This second marriage was also plagued by problems and within two years, the couple was divorced.

Anne was a beautiful girl, but she seemed to have trouble finding her place in the world. She was also an assertive woman and, unlike many wives at that time, not one to simply acquiesce to her husband's demands. When Anne and her husband fought, she could give as she good as she got.

By 1979, Anne and Amy were on their own again and renting an apartment in Scranton. In August of that same year, she applied for a job at Electra-Sonic, a new company that sold energy-efficient furnaces and was hired on as a secretary.

Anne's new boss, and the owner of the company, was thirty-seven-year-old Tom Hodgins, who soon became infatuated with his new secretary. What Tom lacked in looks—he was not all that good-looking—he made up for in charm. For Anne, a young, single mother just coming out of two failed marriages, this older, "successful" businessman's attention was a bit overwhelming, and in no time at all, she was madly in love with him as well.

Within days of their meeting, Tom Hodgins moved into Anne's apartment, and Anne announced that the two planned to marry in November.

I was shocked by the announcement and begged her not do it. "If it's love, it'll last," I told her, but Anne just brushed my worry away. Although I knew the marriage would be a mistake, Anne didn't see it that way. They were in love, she insisted, and on November 21, 1979—only two months after they met—she and Tom were married.

It wasn't difficult to see why Anne was so taken with Tom Hodgins; in the beginning, he treated her like a queen. He gifted her with a huge diamond and a flashy Datsun 280Z, wined and dined her, and was overly generous with his compliments. But Tom was also controlling and demanding and at first, I think Anne was flattered by the attention. "We do everything together," she told me. Soon, however, she realized she could do nothing without him, not even speak privately on the phone. Every time I called her, Tom would picked up the extension and listened to our conversation.

I was wary of him from the beginning. When I look at their wedding pictures today, his eyes appear shifty, and I remember his hugs and kisses seemed insincere. I also caught him in numerous lies during the time he and Anne were married. Later, I would discover that Tom Hodgins was a con-man in everything from his relationships to his business.

He'd been married before, to a woman named Karen who he met while living in Ohio. The couple had at least one child together, but Tom was not faithful to his wife. In 1976, he met Lucille Smith, a married woman with two children, and began an affair with her. Although their relationship was stormy, Tom and Lucille would go on to have a set of twins together, while Tom was still married to Karen.

Eventually, Karen left Ohio and brought her and Tom's son to Pennsylvania, renting a small apartment in the little village of Dundaff. Tom followed her there in 1977, bringing along Lucille and her four children. Incredibly, they moved in with Karen and her son, all of them living together as one "happy" family. After four months of this, Karen apparently had enough and fled back to Ohio, taking her son with her.

Once Karen was gone, Tom and Lucille rented an apartment in the town of Jermyn and lived together until Tom moved in with Anne in August of 1979. Eventually, I would come to learn that Tom was not only a con-man but a bigamist as well, having not bothered to divorce Karen before he married Anne in November.

I knew none of this in the beginning of their relationship, however. What I did know was that Tom had quickly included Anne in his business, listing himself as President of Electra-Sonic and Anne as Secretary-Treasurer.

In October 1979 Tom hired Glenna Laybourne as a secretary at Electra-Sonic, and she and Anne became close friends. Glenna immediately noticed how possessive and jealous Tom was of his wife, but Anne didn't seem to realize it. Just as he did with me, whenever Glenna phoned Anne, Tom would pick up the extension and listen to their conversation. He never seemed to let her out of his sight.

Not long after they married, Tom suggested that as business partners, he and Anne should insure each other's lives. Anne already had a twenty-five-thousand-dollar policy through her agent, James Hicks with Prudential Life Insurance Company. Tom suggested they each take out one-hundred-thousand-dollar policies, and Hicks happily wrote them up. Perhaps Anne had some misgivings. The beneficiary on her smaller policy was still listed in her ex-husband, Michael Revak's name, and not long after she and Tom secured the large policies, Anne called her agent and asked that the beneficiary on the smaller policy be changed. But she did not change it to benefit her new husband, Tom Hodgins, she changed it to benefit her sister, Cathy Green. At the same time, she also asked Hicks about reducing the amount of the one-hundred-thousand-dollar policies.

Anne paid the first months premium on the large polices, and then stopped paying all together. As a result, those two large polices soon lapsed. I have no idea if Tom knew about his, but he did find out about her changing the beneficiary on the small policy and he was decidedly unhappy. "Partners should insure each other, not two other people," he said angrily.

***

Tom had hit on a good idea with his energy-efficient Electra-Sonic furnaces. Soon the units were selling like hotcakes, and the money began rolling in. The company was so busy in fact that the orders for the furnaces far outnumbered the units that had been produced.

One day, local homeowner, Frank Clark, came into the office asking for information, and Tom's pitch was so smooth that Clark immediately purchased one of his furnaces on the spot. Tom delivered a "black box" to Clark's house and cut the water pipes, but neither assembled the furnace nor hooked it up.

Robert Henwood, another local resident, also purchased an Electra-Sonic furnace in October 1979. Henwood put five-hundred dollars down, after which a black box was delivered to his house, and his water pipes cut. Tom told him he'd return to install the unit when Henwood paid the balance on the bill. Henwood paid, but Tom never returned to his house again.

One day, Tom asked fourteen-year-old Chopper, to come down and help him install some of the new furnaces. Chopper went gladly, but when he returned home, he seemed perplexed and shook his head.

"Mom, his furnaces are nothing but black boxes. They have no controls or heat producers."

This was alarming news. I knew that Tom was selling these units daily, and removing the buyer's old furnaces when they were installed. What the hell was he doing? I wondered.

Apparently, what Tom was doing was ripping people off right and left, and it wasn't long before his new secretary, Glenna Laybourne, saw the writing on the wall. The business was quickly failing, and every day she was being barraged with phone calls from irate customers. In December 1979, Glenna quit her job at Electra-Sonic, but securing her last paycheck from Tom Hodgins was like pulling teeth. It took weeks of constant badgering and threats before Tom finally paid her, and once he did, Glenna was happy to be rid of him. She felt bad for Anne, however, and stayed in touch with her as often as she could.

By early 1980, Frank Clark and Robert Henwood were freezing. Tom Hodgins had still not hooked up their new furnaces and worse yet he had taken out their old ones. After repeated phone calls in which both men demanded that Tom either complete the job or return their money each man filed charges against him for "theft by deception."

I found out about Tom's troubles in March 1980 when I walked into the house and saw the local news station airing a segment about fraudulent practices conducted by a firm called "Electra-Sonic." I was shocked, but not surprised—I had already heard the rumors swirling around. Soon, I also found out that Tom had stopped paying the rent on the Connell Building offices where his business was housed and by April, the landlord had evicted him.

Tom was in big trouble, and asked his lawyer, Brian Cali, to represent him on several consumer complaints relating to Electra-Sonic. Tom didn't allow Cali to peruse his books, but he did show the attorney that his bank account hovered at zero dollars. Cali was able to get Tom's hearing postponed until April, at which time Tom was bound over for Grand Jury action. The Grand Jury indicted, and a trial date was set for September 1980.

By this time, there were major problems in Anne and Tom's marriage. Tom had become even more controlling, jealous, and possessive, and Anne, no longer flattered by the attention, sometimes felt as if she couldn't breathe. One day, in the summer of 1980, Anne met Glenna Laybourne at Lackawanna State Park where the two had brought their children to play. Anne related how she and Tom were fighting regularly. A little later, Glenna was shocked to see Tom following and watching his wife from a distance as if stalking her.

"He never lets me out of his sight," Anne said, disgustedly.

Glenna was not the only one who saw Tom's jealousy first-hand. Janet Kalasinski, who had married Anne's ex-husband Stan, got a visit from Tom Hodgins that summer as well. Tom had shown up at her house angry and upset and told Janet that Anne and Stanley were still seeing each other. Janet noticed several scratches along Tom's chest which he told her Anne inflicted during an argument.

"Anne and Stanley are seeing each other," Tom yelled.

"Tom," Janet said, trying to calm him down, "Anne and Stan have a child together. If they communicate at all, it's only for Amy's benefit."

Tom would not be placated, however. He was acting like a wild man and at one point, said to her, "I have a gun, and I'm a member of the Mafia, but believe me, not as a mechanic!" Afterward, his voiced softened but remained icily cold. "I never hit a woman before," he hissed, "but she'll be the first."

Estelle Doherty, Anne's hairdresser, also heard about Tom Hodgins jealousy. In a telephone conversation, Anne complained that she wasn't able to "go out without him because he's so jealous. He's here all the time."

Estelle felt sorry for Anne and advised her to "take Amy and go to your mother's."

***

Years earlier, Tom had saved the life of a man named Jerry Warnero. Warnero had been in a motorcycle accident and Tom, the first person on the scene, had applied a tourniquet and kept the man from bleeding to death. Warnero had never forgotten it, and afterward, the two became good friends. Now, in early August 1980, Tom called Warnero and asked him to go shopping. On August 4, 1980, the two men visited Al Messina, where Tom purchased a small derringer handgun. Tom then asked Jerry if he could make adjustments to the weapon. Anne would be shooting it, Tom explained, and the gun needed to have the pull on the trigger reduced. Warnero agreed, and after making the adjustments, gave Tom two .38 hollow point bullets for the gun.

Four days later, on August 8, 1980, Tom took out another life insurance policy on Anne. This one was in the amount of twenty-five-thousand-dollars but was enhanced with an accidental death clause whereby the face value would double if death occurred from an accident.

***

On Saturday, August 23 Anne spoke with her sister, Cathy and invited her to join her and Tom for "Mom and Dad's anniversary dinner next Sunday." Anne seemed upbeat and told Cathy she was happy because she had her car up for sale and thought she had found a buyer. They were strapped for cash, Anne confided, and Amy needed clothes for school. In the next breath, however, Anne mentioned that the house they were renting was up for sale, and they were seeking a VA loan to buy it.

I had already heard about Anne and Tom's plans to buy the house, but not from Anne. During the second week of August, she and Tom had visited Stan and me at the cottage and while there, Anne and her father talked in the kitchen as Tom and I chatted in the living room. Tom seemed edgy and nervous, and I began to get the distinct impression that he was keeping me occupied so Anne could talk to her father in private. When the two finally left, I confronted Stan.

"What was that all about?"

"She asked for a loan of twenty-five hundred dollars for a down payment on a house."

I was flabbergasted. "How can they get a loan for a house when neither of them is working, and Tom's business is failing?"

Stan shrugged his shoulders, obviously thinking the same thing.

Now, on August 23, I too received a phone call from Anne telling me that she and Tom wanted to take Stan and me out to dinner for our twenty-ninth wedding anniversary.

"That's sweet, honey," I told her, "But you can't afford it."

"Come on Mom," Anne said, "Bring Chopper and we'll celebrate his birthday too."

While we were speaking, the conversation was interrupted by a knock on Anne's door.

"Hold on a minute," Anne said, then added, "It's the police."

Concerned, I told her to go see what they wanted and quickly hung up. Later, I learned that the police were there with a summons for Tom to appear in court for passing bad checks.

One week later, on the morning of Saturday, August 30 Anne sold her car to Sherry Lacone for four-hundred-dollars. According to Sherry, Anne had come outside dressed in a robe and seemed to be in good spirits. In the late afternoon, Tom and his brother, Jimmy went target practicing with two guns; the newly purchased derringer and a muzzle loading handgun. Afterward, Tom, Anne, Jimmy and his girlfriend, Debbie went together to two local town events; the Mayfield Picnic and Pioneer Days in Carbondale, after which, the foursome returned to Jimmy's house where they played cards until around midnight when Tom and Anne left for home.

Only hours later, at 4:05 a.m., I would be awoken at our cottage by the shrill ring of the telephone and life as I had always known it would cease to exist.

CHAPTER FIVE

When Stan and I finally arrived at the hospital and were escorted into the Trauma Room, my worst nightmare came true—one of my children was lying unconscious on the stretcher. Anne was intubated and connected to a respirator. Her head was wrapped in a bandage, and her hands encased in plastic bags.

Rushing to her, I whispered through my tears, "Why didn't you call me? What was so bad in your life that you would be forced to do this?"

Of course, there was no answer, only the steady hum of the respirator as it breathed for my baby. We questioned one the emergency medical technicians who had been on the scene and he told us that when they got to Anne's apartment they found her slumped in a recliner, bleeding from the head and with hands outstretched. "We intubated her, started an IV and gave her Valium, (to prevent convulsions in head and brain injuries), then transported her here to the emergency room," he said solemnly.

When asked about the location of the bullet wound, the EMT informed us that the entrance wound was above the left ear, the exit wound behind the right. That made absolutely no sense to me.

"How is that possible?" I asked. "She's right-handed. She hates guns. She would never do this to herself!"

While we were grilling the EMTs, the police were grilling Tom and Amy, Anne's daughter, both of whom had been in the apartment when Anne supposedly shot herself.

The doctors gave us no hope, telling us the bullet had done massive damage, and Anne would not survive. At 6:30 a.m. she was transported to the Intensive Care Unit where we began our vigil—waiting for her to die. As we settled in the waiting room, mixed emotions began to swirl around us—and the police questioning did not help. They asked us if Anne had been depressed, or if she'd ever done anything like this before?

"No," I insisted. "Anne has a terrible temper, and she's been very upset over money and Tom's failing business."

"Well," one of the officers asked bluntly, "How many times has she tried to kill herself in the past?"

Dumbstruck, I just stared at the man, wondering what he was talking about. Anne wasn't suicidal, I insisted, and she'd never attempted suicide before. "Anne's too vital and vain a person to do anything to herself," I said.

The officer seemed surprised by these revelations. Apparently Tom had already told them that Anne *was* suicidal, a statement I knew to be untrue.

The waiting room was packed. Along with Stan and me, everyone else was there too: Cathy, her husband, Todd and their infant, Kelly. Chopper, Larry, Michael, and Tom's family too, his mother, Ann Nelson, his brother, Jimmy and Jimmy's girlfriend, Debbie. After a short time, Tom arrived from police headquarters, where he had been taken for questioning.

Soon, my mother showed up, and Stan's brother, Larry with his son, Larry Jr. As word spread, other family members arrived and drifted in and out between Anne and us. The only one we were waiting on was our daughter, Aileen who was flying in from Georgia where she was stationed with the Army in the Criminal Investigation Department.

Whenever I went into the ICU to sit with Anne, Tom always joined me and sat on the other side of the bed. After a while, he began to relate to me wild stories of Anne's behavior since their marriage, nine months before. Anne was acting crazy and out of character, Tom said. She'd been dancing around the apartment so wildly that she'd caused a chandelier in the apartment below them to crash right off the ceiling.

Why is he telling me this? I wondered. Did he want me to think that Anne was taking drugs and acting crazy? I didn't believe half of what he was saying—I'd known my daughter for twenty-eight years, and some of the tales he told were beyond belief.

I knew there was no hope, and several hours after Anne was admitted to ICU I spoke with her neurosurgeon, Dr. Platt, and begged him to turn off the respirator.

"Have you considered organ donation?" He asked.

I hadn't thought about that, but I knew it was something Anne would want. Dr. Platt told us that in that case, twenty-four hours had to transpire before they could take Anne off life-support. Time passed infinitesimally slowly. As the family spent time with her in ICU and prayed, we also began comparing notes on what Tom was telling each of us. To some, he said when he and Anne came home that night, Anne found a letter on the porch steps informing them that their bid on the house had been rejected. She got upset and went into the "workroom," and afterward he heard a shot. To others, he said he was checking the children when he heard a shot, and to still others, that he was outside or downstairs "having a smoke." Tom's vacillating stories troubled me, and as time went by, I became more and more convinced that Anne did not do this to herself.

We had not slept for over thirty-six hours, nor had Stan, or I had anything to eat or drink all day. At midnight, we finally left the hospital. When we arrived home and crawled into bed, Stan turned to me, and I took him in my arms. Holding each other, the two of us wept until there were no more tears to cry.

Emotionally spent, I eventually drifted off into a hazy sleep and awoke with the aching thought that "today, we will have to say good-bye to our firstborn." The realization cut a searing pain, unlike anything I had ever imagined.

As soon as we arrived at the hospital and I walked into the ICU, I could see that Anne's condition had deteriorated. Her heart was racing at one-hundred-eighty beats per minute, and her kidneys were pouring out quarts of fluid. Rushing to her, I was distressed and horrified to see brain matter oozing from her head dressing and what appeared to be maggots crawling out of her nose.

Later, when the doctor approached us and again asked about donating her organs, we readily agreed. We knew Anne would be pleased, as organ donation was a subject we had discussed with her previously. Consulting with the Transplant Coordinator, I remember thinking what a tactful and sensitive man he was. At one point, when he explained that an artifact was seen on the last electroencephalogram, Tom, appearing worried and surprised, blurted out, "You mean she's going to live?"

I was horrified at the thought, wondering what kind of life she would have on a respirator and in a vegetative state.

The coordinator explained that another EEG would be taken in six hours, and if that too, was flat, "Anne would be declared brain dead and taken to the operating room to have her organs 'harvested.'"

On September 1, 1980—Labor Day—we all gathered next to Anne's bed and gently kissed her goodbye. At 7:00 p.m. the doctors pronounced Anne dead, and she was transported to the operating room.

One of the greatest comforts in our grief was that our daughter gave life and sight to four other people. Anne's spirit lives on through them. Months later, I was able to contact the Delaware Valley Transplant Center, which informed us that her kidneys had been successfully transplanted, one to a civil engineer and the other to a teacher, both of whom had been able to resume their occupations. Her corneas have gone to two people whose sight has been restored.

The next day, Cathy and Aileen went over to Anne's house and were shocked by what they saw. Dirty dishes littered the sink while leftover food was strewn on the counter. Opening the refrigerator, both girls saw that there hardly any food inside. They knew that wasn't like Anne at all; especially since both Amy, and Tom's young son, Jason, who was only three at the time, were living at the house.

In the living room, the two girls saw blood spatter inside the lampshade, and blood-spattered papers crumpled up on the floor. Cathy took it upon herself to scrub the blood off the table and then, worried that Tom would see, rubbed the lampshade with talcum powder to hide the blood.

***

The days following Anne's death were a blur. My heart ached at the thought of never again seeing my daughter. I couldn't comprehend that I would never see her bounce into the house, laughing and singing—never see her beautiful face and tantalizing smile. I thought about celebrating the holidays—just around the corner—without her. I remembered last Christmas Eve when I told her "It's time to begin your own Christmas traditions," and she said, "As long as I live, Christmas will be at your house." Who could ever have imagined that that would be her last Christmas? From then on, Christmas would always be an especially lonely time.

The days after my daughter's death were also a nightmare of

escalating horrors. After being informed by the county coroner that the body could not be released until after an autopsy—scheduled to be performed by New York Forensic Pathologist, Dr. Dominick DeMaio on Tuesday—we planned the viewing for Wednesday and the funeral for Thursday. After the autopsy, I received a call from Grace Wilks, the funeral director's wife. She informed me that the dress we chose—the one Anne had been married in—didn't fit. Anne had gained too much weight since her wedding.

"Slit it up the back and just lay it on her," I said. Why did I need to know such things?

Later, Grace Wilks called back to tell me, "We may not be able to have an open casket—maggots are exuding out of her nose and mouth."

I was so horrified by the thought, I couldn't speak. Does one really need to know that the process of a loved one's body decay had begun?

On Wednesday, as we all sat on our front porch, we watched the hearse containing Anne's body move slowly past the house. It was then that the reality began to set in. Anne had died. She was never coming home.

It was unreal to see my daughter lying in that casket at the viewing, but she looked more peaceful than I had seen her in a long time. Tom was there, of course, and, my suspicions about him not having abated, I felt distinctly uncomfortable in his presence. Soon, Anne's close friend, Glenna Laybourne arrived. Glenna had worked for Tom and had also been one of the last people to see

Anne alive. As she stood in the doorway of the funeral home, the look of sheer malevolence etching her face stunned me. Even more shocking was what came out of her mouth after she stood and prayed at the casket. Turning to Tom, Glenna hissed, "You son of a bitch—I'll get you for this!"

Apparently, my family and I were not the only ones suspicious of Anne's husband.

Barbara Obelenus, a Susquehanna County magistrate, as well as a good friend, also warned me that Tom was under suspicion for the incident. Our own reservations aside, our minds went into overload. What motive did he have for such a horrendous deed?

We could speculate, of course. When Anne had called the week before to invite us to dinner, I was concerned. The noose was tightening on Tom's business practices, and obviously, Anne was involved, but I tried not to dwell on it right then. I needed to lay my baby to rest first.

Never have I felt as bereft as I did when we bid our last goodbye to Anne in the funeral home. I was so overwrought with emotion that Stan literally had to carry me out. As we stood in the back of the church waiting to proceed behind the casket, I saw Mike Revak, Anne's second husband, in the last pew, but I remember little else. Saying goodbye to my first-born child was the saddest day of my life.

As we trudged up the hill to the cemetery, following the pallbearers carrying the casket, my feet felt heavy-laden, as though filled with sand. Placing one foot ahead of the other became paramount—the most difficult trek of my life.

After the burial, Stan comforted the weeping Tom, and I walked down the hill alone.

I never knew how much a heart could break.

***

Anne's death consumed me. Every day I visited her grave up on the hill in Calvary Cemetery, where she had been placed next to Tom's father, but the discontent never left me. Nor did I get peace visiting there, especially when, only weeks after her death, Tom began dating again. This was shocking enough, but I was even more distressed when I discovered who he was seeing; one of Anne's best friends, Bunny Lyons. Our suspicions regarding Tom had not abated, and the uneasiness we felt with Anne's resting place grew more and more uncomfortable each day.

Tom had been evicted from the Clay Street apartment and had moved to the town of Carbondale. Less than two weeks after Anne's death, I drove by his new place and saw his Cadillac sitting outside, filled with my daughter's belongings. I soon discovered that he was selling off everything Anne owned at a local flea market fifteen miles away. Furious, I confronted him and told him I wanted all of Anne's personal items. Tom agreed, but when he brought me some pictures and trinkets, I realized that he had already sold everything of value, including Anne's jewelry, fur coat, and gold china.

"Where is the rest of her stuff?" I asked.

"The big stuff; the furniture, that's been put in storage," Tom said.

The police had taken the chair Anne died in, but not the blood-splattered lamp that sat on the table next to her. I had thought a lot about that lamp over the past two weeks, and, sure that Tom Hodgin's had murdered my daughter, I wanted the lamp taken into evidence too. I told Tom there were things of Anne's the family might want and asked if I could see what was in storage. Backed into a corner, he reluctantly agreed, so I had Cathy's husband, Todd get the lamp out of storage and take it to the police. After tagging it, they placed it in their evidence room.

I tried to come to terms with Anne's death, but the pain and grief were almost unbearable. People looked at me with pity, and fiends avoided discussing her. Stan, grief-stricken himself, didn't know how to cope either. We were both frustrated with the police, who were not pursuing justice in her case, and occasionally, when I would begin to cry, he would say, "Just stop thinking about it."

Just stop thinking about it. Oh, if only I could. I tried, I truly did. Attempting to come to terms with her demise, I would remind myself of her difficult life. She'd survived two failed marriages, single parenthood, and Amy's constant ear infections, which often resulted in Anne having to stay at home with her. She lost many jobs because of Amy's illnesses, as employers both then and now are often not tolerant of children's sickness.

On September 16, two weeks after Anne died, my daughter,

Cathy met with Tom and his mother, Ann Nelson, at Ann's home in Jermyn. Cathy was the beneficiary on Anne's twenty-five-thousand-dollar life insurance policy and Tom, too, had taken a policy out on her in the same amount. It seemed Tom had attempted to collect on the policy, but his request was turned down "pending investigation." Apparently, Tom had taken a term policy with a low premium which included a two-year "no-pay" suicide clause. When Cathy arrived, Tom immediately began ranting about how Anne's death was an "accidental death" and how he would "hire a pathologist to prove it."

Cathy tried to calm her ex-brother-in-law down, but it did little good. The policy for which she was named beneficiary was expected to be paid without question and Tom obviously thought that wasn't fair. He was terrified because he was facing prison time for the scandal that had erupted over his Electra-Sonic business and had apparently been hoping to use the proceeds from the insurance policy to get him out of the jam.

Ever the con-man, Tom used guilt to convince Cathy to help him out. The two traveled to Attorney Brian Cali's office, and there, Cathy signed papers for a twenty-three-hundred dollar loan, using the insurance policy as collateral. This money was used to pay off Robert Henwood and Frank Clark, who in turn, then dropped their consumer complaint against Tom and Electra-Sonic. In the end, Tom didn't pay for his wife's funeral either; Cathy did, again using the insurance proceeds to do so. After giving her siblings and her parent's one-thousand-dollars each, Cathy put the rest of the insurance money in trust for Anne's daughter, Amy.

To my dying day, I will never forget the grief I felt, and still feel over Anne's death. Never had I understood the pain parents feel upon losing a child, and only time has healed the raw sadness. It is not normal for a parent to outlive their children. The emptiness in my heart on the drive home from the hospital, and for days and months after, was indescribable. At times, chest pains hit me, and I was sure I was having a heart attack. The intense loneliness that engulfs one is never assuaged—a part of one has gone that can never be retrieved.

CHAPTER SIX

The days, weeks, and months after Anne's death passed by in a hazy blur. The holidays that year, only four months after the tragedy, were horrendous. It was a time that should have been filled with happiness and joy, but instead was fraught with heartache, grief and searing pain. Anne should have been there, but she was not.

The manner of Anne's death had been listed as "pending." I knew she had been murdered and it galled me to think that Tom Hodgins was going to get away with it. He had picked up his life as if Anne's death had been nothing more than a blemish upon it. While my family and I were consumed by grief and struggled to make it through each day, Tom went on with his life, selling off Anne's belongings and making plans to marry Bunny Lyon. In fact, he and Bunny wed only six weeks after Anne's death and immediately left the area and moved to Florida.

In March, things at work came to a head when, after a sleepless night because of a midnight emergency Cesarean Section, I was so exhausted, I asked another nurse in the operating room if I was okay to make decisions.

"You know Anne, it might be wise to see a psychiatrist," she said.

With that, the full force of my grief gushed forth, and I began hopelessly weeping—in fact, I wept for two whole days. Unable to drive myself home, my son came and literally carried me into the car and once home, I lay on the couch, keening.

I felt I would never recover from this horrible pain and grief. After a week's stay at home—and with the aid of therapy, anti-depressants, sleeping pills and upbeat music—I made a decision to find another place of employment. I was bitter. I had ten weeks of sick leave saved up, but mental illness and depression are not considered sicknesses. Instead, the chief nurse anesthetist called to say, "Perhaps you should go on an *unpaid* leave of absence."

I decided to apply for a job with the Susquehanna Anesthesia Affiliates in Endicott, New York—and was hired on at Wilson Hospital in Johnson City.

About a month after starting my new job, in May 1981, Stan began complaining about pain in his knee.

"Damn arthritis is acting up again," he said.

I thought he was probably right, but the pain did not subside. In fact, it grew worse. By June, when he was limping terribly and could no longer walk without the aid of a cane, we were both worried. Stan was stubborn, however, and it wasn't until early July that he finally agreed to see a doctor. He was sent to St. Joseph's Hospital for x-rays where it was determined that the pain was not arthritis but a sarcoma, one of the fastest growing of all tumors. My husband had cancer!

The diagnosis was a blow that shook me to the core and shattered any semblance of progress I had made since Anne's death. Why was this happening? This can't be happening. Not now. It was happening, however, and I would have to deal with it come what may. I didn't know how to handle the mass of emotion that continually swirled within my mind and body and it was at this time that I began to keep a journal.

July 21, 1981

Today it's been one week since we found out Stan has cancer. To know so much about medicine and have it happen to your own is dreadful. How can he cope with this? How can I help him cope? He's not a fighter, and I feel so much time has gone by that it's too late for any treatment to work. Larry and his intended, Kelly, took Marilyn and Nancy to the hospital to see him and I went to Mass and then visited Anne's grave and talked to God. I can't visualize life without him—his sense of humor, his gentleness, his quiet strength. Oh God, Why—Why—Why? He has never been mean to anyone—why must he suffer so? 'I will lift up mine eyes to the hills, from whence cometh my salvation. My help cometh from the Lord.' After a long time, a message came to me that 'what will be, will be,' and I came home more peaceful. God and I are having some long conversations these days."

Stan was admitted to Wilson Hospital in Johnson City, New York, where I worked, and where he underwent a biopsy of the left femur. I was worried sick, and my fears increased when the doctor told me, "It doesn't look too good, but we'll know more when the biopsy report comes back."

We would spend eight weeks in limbo waiting for that report, but on the assumption that Stan had an osteo-sarcoma his oncologist decided to treat him with twenty-one rounds of radiation and two chemotherapy administrations, later discerning he had a chondrosarcoma.

My life was spinning out of control and I felt helpless to stop it. Anne had only been gone ten months, my husband had cancer, and I had just begun a new job sixty miles from home. The doctors wanted to amputate Stan's leg as part of his treatment, but he adamantly refused.

July 24, 1981

Today, Stan had a Samson rod inserted operatively in his femur. The doctors had convinced him that this was a preferred treatment, along with radiation and chemotherapy, but as I was traveling home tonight, a thought occurred to me with horror, "They've spread the cancer by inserting the rod—they've not removed it!!!" Cathy came up to be with me, and after reacting from the anesthesia, Stan cried out, 'I thought this was going to relieve the pain!' Knowing how much pain cancer patients suffer, I cried inside for him. How can he survive the disillusionment of radiation and chemotherapy? If only I could take the suffering for him. Oh God, I love him so much! He's been my only love for thirty years.

Every day I stopped to visit Stan on my way into the operating room. He was just down the hall at the hospital and I'd take my coffee and lunch breaks with him. After my shift ended at 3:30, I'd stay with him for several more hours before driving the sixty-five miles home.

August 2, 1981

The girls and I went to the chicken barbecue at Kennedy Park and then drove up to Johnson City to Wilson Hospital. Stan was very depressed when we got there, but soon, his brother, Larry, and sister, Marilyn and our son, Larry, and his fiancée, Kelly, arrived to visit, and Stan actually laughed at Larry's description of himself as a "raisin" at their Halloween party last year. Cathy and Todd arrived later and brought the children. Stan loves those babies of Cathy and Todd's so much.

August 3, 1981

Walked over to see Stan at lunchtime and he was in good spirits, except for having talked to Dr. O'Hare, whom he can't stand. In the afternoon, they wanted to transfer him to the orthopedic floor—he doesn't want to move, and he and I had words. He thinks I'm trying to control his decisions and life. His anger made me back off—he needs to be needed and in control—so, from now on, the decisions are his. Chopper had the car inspected and bought tires and got the car fixed (a bad day financially) and tonight took the trash to the dump. Marilyn (she was twelve-years-old then) *had prepared a nice chicken and dumpling dinner, with fresh sweet corn, which we all truly enjoyed. "Pieface," a CB radio friend of Stan's, called and volunteered to take him for his radiation treatments. How upset we were that those treatments would be delayed another week by the surgery, until he heals. We feel we're* losing valuable time—it's been three weeks since we found out he has a tumor and no real treatment yet! Don't even see the lake these days, for I leave early in the morning, and don't return until 6:00 or 7:00 o'clock. Feel like my whole life has been spent in hospitals and now it's too close to home. And how Stan hates hospitals!!! Says he's coming home tomorrow.

August 4, 1981

Stan appeared to be more like his old self today. He-went to Physical Therapy and learned how to crutch walk, but did no weight bearing. After lunch, he washed and shaved. Talked to Dr. Whiting, his oncologist, who seemed to be a very sincere, gentle person—hopeful about starting radiation on Monday. But after seeing Stan getting out of his wheelchair and into bed, the doctor said, 'Better plan on going home over the weekend.' Stan can't really move that leg without a lot of pain so he keeps it still.

August 5, 1981

Today he was really great—asked, "Where've you been?" when I came into his room, though, I couldn't get him out walking. He's gone a whole week without bathing—since he can't, and won't, ask the nurses to do so, I gave him a bath, changed his pajamas and socks. He refused Physical Therapy today—"I know how to walk steps and crutch walk." Bill Doolittle came up to see Stan.

August 6, 1981

Stan came home to the cottage today. He never spoke on the drive home, but was very gregarious when Patti and Gary Sparks, Bill *and Bernetta Doolittle and his sister Betty and her husband, Jim Powderly, visited. He laughed so much all afternoon and evening, it was a treat to see him enjoying himself. They regaled us with stories of what really happened the night of the plane crash the night before we met!*

The following Monday, Stan prepared to drive to Lourdes Hospital in Binghamton to begin his radiation treatments.

August 12, 1981

Stan called me late this afternoon, to Lourdes. "Something snapped in my leg as I was dressing to come up to Lourdes." He had come up to start his radiation, with Bill Doolittle accompanying him. When I rushed across town to Lourdes, I found him crying with pain. He had been sitting in a wheelchair for over three hours in the emergency room! The nurses told me Dr. Kim was upstairs operating. I forced the nurses to call him in the O.R. and he ordered an X-Ray of the leg, Demerol for the pain, and had him admitted. The femur has broken around the rod insertion! I get so upset. The nurses don't see him not moving because of the pain—I fear a thrombus, but would sudden death be preferable to the slow agony of this horror?

August 19, 1981

Am getting more exhausted by the day—last week after Stan was admitted to the hospital, I cried all the way home. The girls are alone at the lake, and I worry constantly about them. To see Stan in tears breaks me up—he's in such pain—I feel so hopeless, and helpless! I don't know whether he's finally grieving for Anne or in such terrible pain it reduces him to tears, or whether he can't stand the thought of "cancer." After taking care of so many people all these years, I can only beg the nurses and doctors—none of whom seem to communicate with each other—to do something! His sister, Marilyn, either calls, or comes up to see him every day. I stop over to see him every afternoon and stay for hours. By Sunday he was in such a depression, he cried constantly. He refused to move to the orthopedic floor where he might get better care. I'm so frustrated by the lack of nursing care he gets—is it because he refuses everything: needles, turning, P.T.—or because they just don't care? He did get out of bed to go to the bathroom.

The doctors don't even agree on his care—one says to move, the others, O'Hare, Coene, and Kim don't seem to know what the other is saying! Do they really know how little activity he has, sitting up in that bed, with the leg growing larger every day? The dressing was removed this week, and he's on medication every four hours, but the leg is so swollen! Gave him a complete bed bath for he hadn't washed in a week.

August 20, 1981

Tomorrow is our 30th wedding anniversary and, after taking a shower, I sat up in bed reading through the Scranton Times, as I always do. Perusing through the columns listing homes for sale for non-payment of taxes, I discovered with dismay that our home is among them!!!

(Stan had neither paid the last two year's taxes, nor told me, so I

told Chopper to gather up Stan's papers from his dresser drawer and take them up to the hospital to find the bills, for I will have to go personally to pay them.)

What a way to spend your anniversary! Where will I get $800 in three weeks? When I came home, there was a bouquet of flowers on the table—from Stan—with the bill beside it!!! The card said, "Love ya, Me," as he's signed all his missiles over the years. Went over to Bernetta's to get Marilyn and Nancy--thank God for good friends!

August 21, 1981

Our 30th wedding anniversary. The phone rang at 11:00 o'clock, as we were getting ready to go up to the hospital, and it was Stan, crying because the doctor had just come in and told him the cancer has spread. His sister Marilyn had sent up a lovely tablecloth, and had arranged for the dietary department to send up a dinner for all of us, but we just sat there in silence picking at the food. God, will we ever smile again? Today was the last time we'll ever celebrate an anniversary together.

How good it is not to know what our futures hold, for on that happy day thirty years ago, though it rained, could we ever have conceived of this kind of anniversary?

***

One day flowed into another, marred by varying degrees of hope, sadness, frustration with the doctors, and profound grief. I knew Stan was dying. I had no one to talk to and was running on pure hope with all my tormented thoughts—worries about how I would care for the children, how I would survive on one income, and constant anger about the care Stan was receiving. Each day I lived to see what his emotional state was—mine was reflected on the journey home. Never have I wept so much in my life. The Irish are said to "have their kidneys right behind their eyeballs," and never more than during that period of my life had that been so true! Though I held it together during the day, I often cried the sixty-five miles to home.

One afternoon, changing into my loafers from my O.R work shoes, I reached into my locker and pulled out one brown and one navy blue shoe which I'd grabbed in the darkened closet that morning. I did an embarrassed shuffle down the corridor, trying to hide my feet as I walked into Stan's room.

"What're you doing with one blue and one brown shoe on?" Stan asked.

Without missing a beat, I replied, "I have a matched set at home in the closet." After a good laugh and visit, I crept down the back stairs, hoping no one would notice!

As harried as my personal life might have been, when I walked into the operating room at work, I put all thoughts of my tragic circumstances on hold. I performed on autopilot, otherwise I could not have continued to administer anesthesia. I prayed to God daily to guide me in my care of His patients.

September 1, 1981

Today I traveled to Scranton to the Courthouse with $800 in my purse to pay the taxes. When I stepped up to the counter with the cash and the tax bill, the clerk informed me, "We can't take cash, Ma'am, only a certified check or money order."

With horror at the prospect of losing our home, I asked angrily, "Why not? This is legal tender in the United States!"

"We can't be responsible for cash in the courthouse over the weekend."

I raged and cried at him, telling him. "I spend every night with my dying husband. I can only come here on Saturday. I can't get to a bank because I work 7:00 to 3:30. I am not going to lose my house, too. I am not leaving this office until someone takes my cash! Who knows what the next week will bring?"

Finally, one of the managers stepped up and, with compassion, stated, "I'll be responsible for the money, Ma'am." He took the cash and gave me a receipt. What other indignities must I endure?

September 30, 1981

It has been a long time since I wrote in this diary—days of pure frustration, profound sorrow, and grief. To see Stan failing daily and trying to present a happy face to him, when inside I'm screaming! Meanwhile, the girls are alone every day until I get home, sometimes not until 7:00 p.m. Chopper (who had joined the Navy and come home after three weeks when he could not get into Radar School and was discharged) is out drinking and driving, who knows where, and I constantly worry about the future without Stan. My grief is so intense sometimes that I've started to pray just to get through the next hour, for I can't imagine life without him. I *talk to no one about him, except for phone calls to the children. Some of the girls at work ask about him, but I rarely have time to discuss his treatment, for I spend all my spare time over in his room and arrive home at night with such mixed emotions. If only I had someone who could really share my grief! Marilyn has something cooked for me but I can hardly get anything down.*

October 1, 1981

Today he had his whole left leg amputated. After more than seven hours in the operating room, twenty-five units of blood, and twelve units of plasma, he was more dead than alive when he arrived in ICU. How my heart aches to see this strong man, who'd never had a sick day in his life, so pale and vulnerable, lying there with tubes in every orifice, barely responsive. His sister, Marilyn, and Cathy remained with me all day. How I hurt, to see the void in the bed where his leg had been! He, thankfully, was sedated, and I'm sure not even aware that we were there. His sister, Pat and Frank came from Connecticut to see him.

The week before, when Stan discovered he was to have his whole leg amputated, he was furious, unhappy, and thoroughly disgusted. He was wondering if I would still love him—as though I fell in love with his legs—and so I got on the phone and called the American Cancer Society and begged them to ask someone who had had this particular operation to come and talk to him. When I told him that a female who had had the operation would be coming to discuss it with him, he screamed at me, "I don't need anyone to talk to—not a female, and certainly not a stranger! The doctors will tell me what it's like to have a leg amputated!" I rushed out of the hospital and drove home in tears, begging God to help him and me! (I later learned his roommate chastised him saying, "She's only trying to help you get through this.")

The next day, uncertain of how I would find him, I was late getting to the hospital room and he was sitting up waiting for me. He couldn't contain his eagerness.

"You'll never guess what happened today," He said excitedly.

"What?" I asked.

In a rush, he told me about a young man named John Soloway, who had also had his leg amputated. John had approached him in the Physical Therapy room while Stan was lying on the cart, waiting to be lifted into the Hubbard tank (which was done daily to prevent bedsores). John, knowing that Stan was about to have the same operation he had, had told Stan, "How easy it is to wear the prosthesis, although I only wear mine for weddings."

John described for him the "phantom pain" one experiences after losing a limb, and seeing this young man who had undergone the surgery in June (in addition to lung surgery and an appendectomy) gave Stan such hope that he said to me, "When are they going to do it? Call the doctor and let's get on with it."

I called Dr. Kim to inform him that Stan had made his decision, and we arranged to transport him over to Wilson from Lourdes where he'd been admitted in August, because Stan wanted Dr. Choi, one of my employers, to give him the anesthesia.

I was incredulous that an answer to my prayer had come overnight, and I questioned Stan about it, asking, "What was John doing in Physical Therapy?"

"Having his ears tested," Stan replied.

To this day I consider John Soloway, our personal angel. For Stan had a total change of attitude. He never cried again and did his best to get better.

(In December 1998, I was able to contact this young man and thank him. Twenty years later, he is still alive, for he had undergone some radical chemotherapy in California, where his tumor was discovered while a young man in the service. He told me that, "I had my ears tested the day I talked to Stan because the chemotherapy could have damaged my hearing." He is presently on disability, the father of five children, and after talking to him, I cried, thinking about Stan's treatment. Stan, too, should have had the leg amputated as soon as the tumor was found in July. By September, he'd undergone twenty-one radiation, and one chemotherapy treatment, compromising his immune system. Dr. Whiting, his oncologist, admitted to me, in September that the pathologists had made a mistake. They had treated Stan for osteosarcoma, when, in fact, he had a chondrosarcoma, a diagnosis I found in the book of internal medicine—based on his symptoms—the second week after he had been admitted to Wilson Hospital.)

Every day, Stan became worse; his appetite waned with the

radiation, chemotherapy, and surgery. Every day I would find out what was available in the cafeteria, and often brought him food from there, thinking it might stimulate his taste buds, but it didn't. Day by day he began resorting to only the Ensure supplement with ice cream added. One day he spit out what he had taken in his mouth, and said, "It tastes like wood." At this point, discouragement about his eventual recovery began to overcome me, for if one doesn't eat, one cannot live.

October 10, 1981

Today, on a glorious fall day in the Union Dale Presbyterian Church, in a simple ceremony, Larry and Kelly Foster were married. As I was escorted down the aisle by Chopper, I could hardly contain my tears. People might have thought they were for the children—and they were—but it was also an acceptance of being alone for all the upcoming events in my children's lives. For Stan was not beside me. Kelly wore a simple gown and veil, and the reception afterward at the Montdale Country Club was a beautiful culmination of their eleven-year courtship. I particularly remember the outdoor photos by the shores of the pond behind the Club, with the red, gold, and orange bedecked trees. After the reception, the family and wedding party traveled to the hospital to see Stan, and he tried hard to rejoice with them. We brought champagne and cookies to the staff and it was quite a sight with the bride and groom in their finery and the whole family accompanying them.

November 19, 1981

Today, Stan went into the operating room; I think, hoping to die. He has failed so. His Dad died on this day in 1947, and so he chose this day for his stump to be debrided. I bid him a cheerful farewell, then sat and cried for the hours he was in there. Last Sunday, I walked in while his nurse, Terry Anderson, was dressing his blackened, deteriorating stump and I stood outside the curtain with horror. I had never seen anything like his wound in all my nursing career! She took over an hour to dress it and I could well see why the doctors had to do the debridement under anesthesia. I knew then that Stan's days are numbered. While he was in the operating room, I went to the chapel and prayed that he wouldn't die on the table—that his family could be with him. Cathy and Todd come often to see him, but he has ordered a "No Visitors" sign on the door, for he says he wants "only you to see me." How ironic, that all our married years, when I desired to be alone on a trip or vacation with him, he chose not to. Now, in these harrowing, mournful, emotional days, he wants only me! I need to take care of our legal affairs and don't know how. Suppose he'd died on the table and I were in an accident on the way home? He came out of the surgery alive—not much more than that though.

With great trepidation after writing this, I got up the courage and had a lawyer come to the hospital and make out wills for both of us. I had been fearful about it, for it indicated to Stan that he was dying, but he accepted it with his usual grace and aplomb, and deeded over his share of the Crystal Lake property to his sisters and brother.

December 10, 1981

I exited off route 81 and the Volvo started clunking—I knew it had to do with the fan belt—it was blowing and snowing so hard, I could hardly see to drive, all I did was pray just to get home. God, what else can happen? I called Mike, who came from Union Dale and diagnosed the problem as a broken fan clutch "Get one tomorrow up in Vestal, and I'll put it on," he told me.

Stan lapsed into a coma last night, so I didn't come home—I stayed with him, and slept in the chair, then walked over to the operating room and worked the day. But tonight, I had to come home to see to the girls. Chopper took off for Texas last Saturday, after a shouting match. He came home and said, "Someone threw a beer bottle into the rear window of the Subaru while Pat and I were riding on the Simpson Road." I was so heartbroken to be going through the grieving, anger and frustration with Stan's care, and then to come home to Chopper's antics. In retrospect, he was responding in his own way to all the grief, anger and inability to do anything about the inadequate investigation of Anne's murder and the illness of his "best buddy." The day after he left for Texas, my sister-in-law Marilyn asked me, when I arrived at the hospital, "How's Chopper?" And I replied angrily, "He left for Texas today," and I have to admit that I was relieved of worrying about what he was going to do next.

Always in the back of my mind was the fact that my ten and twelve year old daughters were alone sixty-five miles away, (today I would be charged with child abuse and neglect) *and I was so torn—trying to spend as much time with my dying husband plus taking care of my responsibility to the girls and Chopper. When I arrived home, Marilyn informed me that Chopper had been "unable to get a job in the oilfields, and so he and another fellow had driven directly back from Texas and he's now sleeping." I woke him to wrap the broken Subaru window in plastic, so I can drive it tomorrow. Stan can't last much longer, but he did come out of the coma today.*

December 11, 1981

The day began with my being unable to get the Subaru started, so had to call 'Pieface,' Stan's CB radio friend, to drive me up to the hospital. Stayed with Stan all day. He fell into another coma tonight and, at 3:00 A.M., the nurses roused me as I dozed beside him and told me to "call the family." He was in so much pain, his blood pressure reading 70/50 and his pulse barely discernible. I've told the doctors he's to be kept comfortable but he takes only oral medicine—Dilaudid—and hasn't had any. I don't know how he's survived this long. He's drunk only Ensure with ice cream for weeks. Cathy, Todd, Marilyn, Michael and Chopper came up and we called the Red Cross to have Aileen brought home from her Army post in Georgia. Kelly called Larry to come home from Bermuda where he's on a project. Sister Aileen and Russ came over from Vestal to see him, and their pastor, Monsignor Giblin, gave him the last rites. After spending the day with Stan, during which time he was entirely conscious, and various members of the family drifting in and out of the room, we decided to go to supper in shifts. After Mike and I returned and others had gone to supper, I was sitting beside Stan, and he pushed forward and said "I can't breathe." As I held my hand on his fluttering pulse and elevated the back of the bed, his heart stopped. I sat there with my hand in his as each member of the family walked into the room. Ever the nurse, I tried to find his dentures to put them in his mouth, and couldn't find them—apparently he'd thrown them in the trashcan.

After taking care of the death certificate and other paper work to have his body transported back to Pennsylvania for the funeral, Mike drove us home.

Uncle Larry had gone to the Wilkes-Barre airport to get Aileen, and just as her plane landed, someone called her to tell her "Daddy just died." It was 6:00 p.m., and the love of my life was gone. Alert, conscious and surrounded by his family, he died the most peaceful death I have ever witnessed.

Later that night, the whole family gathered around the kitchen table, and we planned the funeral for Monday, with a viewing on Sunday. Since Stan had been one of the charter members of the Forest City Ambulance Association, a councilman, President of the Lewis Lake Cottagers' Association, and former President of the Forest City Taxpayers' Association, there was a tremendous outpouring of support with flowers, food, visits and phone calls. His co-workers from IBM attended the funeral, in a body, and were so kind to my family and me. They had been so attentive during his illness, personally showering him with visits and gifts and hand-carrying his weekly paycheck. Astounded by the flowers and other "feminine" type of remembrances, I asked him once, "Who are your co-workers that they're giving you these?"

Stan had replied, "I work with fourteen females!"

Numb with grief, I was sure I was not going to survive another funeral. The loneliness overwhelmed me, and as I sat in the church, realizing that Stan would never be at my side again, I prayed just to get through another hour.

Taking one day at a time, I survived. If I thought I'd been lonely in Norfolk, this had that beat by a country mile! Cathy and Todd visited every Sunday with their precious girls, and I recall Todd, almost with disgust, asking, "When are you going to stop crying?"

The holidays were right around the corner—again—and I remember thinking, Christmas will never be the same. Anne had been gone for last Christmas, Stan would be gone for this one, and on this same day four years ago, Larry's girlfriend had been killed on his motorcycle. I'm sure it's a sorrowful time for him, as well, and I recall him telling me once, "Everyone deals with grief in his own way."

Not long after Anne's death, Sister Carleen told me, "God never sends us more than we can handle." At the time, I retorted, somewhat angrily, "Well, you know what? He can forget me for a while!!" I thought about that a lot during those days and wondered why all of this had happened.

***

Does anyone know how to handle grief? The days after Stan's death were something we all had to get through, and in retrospect, I have to say that having my faith and my family was the dearest and best comfort I could have. After our marriage, we took all the changes in our lives—births, new jobs, and moves—with equanimity. Though one of the requirements for my life's partner was that he be a Catholic, which Stan was, a problem arose when he refused to attend church, preferring to sleep in on Sundays. Realizing that this was his decision, I arose every Sunday and took the children to Mass where they were all baptized, confirmed and received Holy Communion. Four of our children were married in the Catholic Church, but only two attend Sunday services today, which grieves me. I truly believe that the support of a parish community in times of joy, and especially in times of grief, is inestimable. Jesus says, "Wherever two or more of you are gathered in my name, I am with you." Therefore, I was relieved to find that Stan returned to his faith while hospitalized at Lourdes. He had gone to both confession and communion before he died, and in his possessions from the hospital, I found a prayer book which he apparently used while a patient.

The days after Stan's death were hard ones. I forced myself to go through the actions of daily life, but tears would suddenly erupt over the slightest thing; if I smelled the shaving lotion he had worn, or heard one of our favorite songs on the radio. People looked at me with pity, not knowing what to say, and afraid to mention Stan or Anne for fear of bringing forth more tears. During those ensuing months, deadening sleep was all I looked forward to, yet I began having some serious insomnia.

It was one of the most bitter, bone-chilling winters I remember, and as I drove to Endicott every day I fretted about how I would manage. The girls and Chopper needed tending, household chores needed to be done, and there was no time for grieving. "Just do it," became my forte.

There were no grief counselors, nor would I have had time for them if there had been, but I did attend one or two meetings of the "Compassionate Friends" and received some comfort from others who shared my pain. I never returned, though, after I talked to one mother whose son had been killed by a hit and run driver in Massachusetts. He husband had simultaneously been diagnosed with a sarcoma of the foot and had it amputated at Sloan Kettering in New York, but he survived. I was happy that he had, of course, but it was still agonizing for me to think that this woman, who had lost a child and whose husband had cancer, was the lucky one.

Having just started my new job in May, with the Susquehanna Anesthesia Affiliates in New York, my main consideration was to gather my children together in that location. But I decided not to take the girls out of school so soon after their father's death. They had had enough upheaval in their lives; they didn't need anymore. Instead, I continued to commute the one-hundred-thirty mile round trip to Vandling, until the following August, when I bought a house in Endwell, New York and enrolled the girls in the Union-Endicott School system.

Chopper chose to remain with Cathy, whose marriage had begun to crumble. As she and Todd began divorce proceedings, there were times when my stress level felt like it was 100 on a scale of 0—10. But hey, what was a move, a new job, selling the old house, buying a new one, and facing another divorce in the family, compared to the previous two years' occurrences?

The Walsh Family. L-R Aileen, Mom, Florence Pop and Anne

Anne Walsh Third Grade

Anne Walsh Nurses Training 1950

Anne and Stan November 1950

Stan on our honeymoon 1951

Stan Coar 1951

Our daughter Anne Graduation 1969

Mrs. Anne Kalasinski

Tom Hodgins

The last Coar family photo, May 1979. Front row L-R Marilyn, Anne, Nancy, and Aileen. Back Row L-R Stan, Mike, Cathy, Chopper, Larry and Anne.

Mr. and Mrs. Andrew Crowley August 1997

Anne's 80th Birthday, Seated L to R Aileen, Anne, Cathy. Standing L-R Anne's daughter Amy, Larry, Andy, Nancy and Chopper.

Nancy's wedding. The last Coar Family Photo with Spouses and grandchildren. Standing L-R Mike, Matt, Jay, Aileen, Maureen, Larry, Marilyn, John, Nick, Nancy, Kelly, Cathy, Jen, Michelle, Chopper and Amy. In front, Micah D, Elijah, Anne and Andy.

Anne Coar Crowley Today

CHAPTER SEVEN

For months after Stan's death, I was numb. I had lost my daughter and my husband in less than fifteen months. It was a bleak and cold winter, and I was simply going through the motions. Working every day, driving the one-hundred-thirty mile round trip to New York daily, and trying to help my young children cope with their loss. In addition to my grief, the thought that Tom Hodgins was getting away with murder infuriated me.

In January, only a month after losing Stan, a recovery room nurse asked me, "Did they ever do anything more in your daughter's death?"

"No," I replied, shaking my head. In fact, in April 1981, just before Stan became ill, we had our one and only visit with the District Attorney, Ernest (Ernie) Preate who informed us that the police had done nothing more in their investigation and thus no progress had been made. "If I could just get someone like Quincy," I told the nurse, "I'm sure we could find Tom guilty."

"You should call Stuart James," she said.

When I indicated that I didn't know who that was, she proceeded to tell me that Stuart James was a former Wilson employee who had struck out on his own as a crime and blood spatter specialist.

For two years, I had focused on Stan's illness, but Stan was gone now, and I realized that it was time to turn my attention to

Anne's murder. For that's what everyone believed; that Tom Hodgins had murdered my daughter.

I decided to call Stuart James, and after contacting him by phone, he came to my home in Vandling which had not yet been sold. I informed him of my suspicions: the twenty-five thousand dollar life insurance policy, Tom's marrying Bunny Lyons six weeks after Anne's death and then the two of them fleeing to Florida. I also told him that Bunny's father had bought Anne's furniture, which she had owned when Tom married her on November 21, 1979.

Stuart James agreed to look into the case, and after paying him five hundred dollars, he began investigating. He contacted the Scranton police and requested both their reports and the chair and table lamp from Anne's shooting. Then Stuart James began doing his own study of the evidence.

Convinced now that my daughter had been murdered, I wanted her to have no connection with Tom Hodgins. That included her final resting place, which he had chosen among his own deceased relatives. Going into court, I told my story to the judge who immediately granted me an exhumation order, and in the summer of 1982, I had Anne brought back to Forest City and laid to rest.

The District Attorney had given us no hope, thus Stuart James became my final hope.

After James perused the police reports and examined the evidence in his own lab, he issued his report in which he concurred with my suspicions. "Yes," Stuart James told me, "Anne had been murdered. Not only that, but there was clear evidence that the body had been moved after death."

This didn't surprise me, since I knew Tom had murdered Anne and set the scene to make it look like a suicide. I felt vindicated by James' words, but getting a cause of death changed on a death certificate was no easy task. It took numerous conferences and multiple phone calls to former Wayne County coroner, Robert Jennings and Corning Community College Forensics professor, James Chapman. They, along with Stuart James, each agreed that the first thing that needed to be done was for Anne's body to be exhumed and another autopsy performed. This time, by some of the top forensic pathologists in the country.

Everyone also agreed that publicity would not hurt, and so I began giving interviews. I was interviewed on television with Bob Reynolds which generated renewed interest in the case. Subsequently, we received permission to exhume Anne's body. This time, along with Dr. Dominick DeMaio who originally performed the autopsy, Dr. Michael Baden from New York, and Dr. Halbert Filinger from Philadelphia would be in attendance as well.

District Attorney Ernie Preate was decidedly unhappy with me and my determination to bring my daughter's killer to justice. Not only did he claim that I should be responsible for paying for these high-priced pathologists, but we engaged in several shouting matches as well.

"Why should we pursue this," Preate screamed at me on the phone one day, "You're a New York state resident."

"I still own property in Lackawanna County, and I'm a taxpayer!" I shouted back. (My Vandling home and two lots had yet to be sold.)

Even more alarming was the fact that, according to a telephone lineman, District Attorney Preate had placed a tap on my telephone.

This was an election year, and Preate liked neither the untoward publicity of an unsolved case, nor the unwarranted expense of a second autopsy and subsequent trial. His political ambitions did not stop at the Lackawanna County District Attorney's office—he was subsequently elected Pennsylvania's State Attorney General and had aspirations of becoming governor. But he was later tried and convicted of mail fraud and sent to jail.

Despite his unhappiness, on March 1, 1983, I walked into my home to see on the local news, Anne's coffin being lifted out of the grave. Although relieved that things were finally moving in her case, I was greatly grieved and angered too. Was this never to end? Why had not a proper police investigation been conducted immediately following her murder? Was Anne never to be allowed to rest in peace?

The autopsy was performed at Scranton State Hospital and present with Doctors Baden, Filinger and DeMaio, was William Sweeney, the Lackawanna County coroner. At this autopsy,

Doctors Baden and Fillinger concurred that this was a homicide and finally, the manner of death was changed on Anne's death certificate from 'pending, 'to homicide. It was a tremendous relief.

***

Since moving into our new home the previous August, I was thankful that I no longer had to travel so far for work, but I was lonely too. The girls had quickly formed friendships in the neighborhood and soon joined the Union-Endicott marching band, which frequently occupied their after-school and evening hours.

Re-opening Anne's case was a stressful time. I did not want it to consume my life, and I needed some adult companionship, so I decided to join the local Square Dance Club. There, I met a partner who was not exactly an ideal square dancer. He wore hiking boots, and when ordered by the caller to "do-si-do," often headed for the nearest door or window. Quite honestly, he thoroughly freaked everyone out in the square. Dancing with him was stressful—exactly what I did not need—and I soon asked the caller to introduce me to another partner. On June 4, 1983, I received a phone call from a fellow who described himself as "six feet tall with blue eyes, and a big nose." He asked me to be his partner and told me his name was Andy Crowley.

Sometimes, people cross your path and make a difference in your life. Such a person in my life is Andrew Crowley. We began dancing that summer, advancing our skills, graduating from basic to advanced, and then to plus levels. Wearing matching outfits, we became members of the Penny-Promenaders Square Dancing Club in Waverly, New York. Meeting people to socialize with, and getting some exercise was my salvation. I needed to reduce my stress level with the pending investigation into Anne's death, as well as get on living after experiencing the two deaths so recently in my family.

Having Andy as a partner was a distinct plus, for he was quiet, unassuming, deeply religious, and one of the kindest men I have ever been fortunate enough to meet. He is also a great listener, which I truly needed at that time in my life. (I later found out Andy was hard-of-hearing, which has given us some funny moments, especially when he thinks he hears me say one thing, and I've said something else.)

We began to travel to statewide club dances, taking the girls with us, who thought us a bunch of old fogies!

I discovered that Andy loved to travel, and we took many weekend get-a-ways together with the girls; to the Adirondacks, the Thousand Islands and other places, each a memorable experience since I had never traveled or taken the children on vacation anywhere. Those trips made me remember something Stan said to me while he was in the hospital. "When I get out of here, we're going to travel." It was heartbreaking to think about because the only traveling Stan did was to the cemetery in a box.

***

On July 18, 1983, after a meeting between the District Attorney's office and the pathologists, Tom was finally arrested and brought to Scranton from Twin Oaks, Pennsylvania where he was then residing. He was charged with murder in the third degree and I can remember exactly where I stood in the kitchen when the phone call from a reporter came with news of his arrest. My rejoicing knew no bounds—but this was only the beginning of more heartache and distress.

Five days later, *The Sunday Times* ran the following editorial.

"If it hadn't been for the determination and perseverance of Mrs. Anne Walsh Coar, law enforcement officials might still be classifying the death 34 months ago of Mrs. Anne Coar Hodgins of Scranton, as suspicious, and possibly a suicide. But thanks to a combination of maternal intuition and the work of a private investigator she hired, police have obtained evidence that Mrs. Hodgins was murdered and have arrested her husband, Thomas, as the killer. The case is not one that Scranton police or District Attorney Preate can boast about, although Preate claimed just before the arrest, that "We were never fooled from the beginning." Yet, police had evidence hours after the woman was shot in the head that indicated "the bullet might have been fired by her husband." Deputy Police Chief Frank Karam expressed his concern that Mrs. Coar had lost confidence in local authorities and felt she had to engage a private investigator. He also indicated that there hadn't been sufficient communication between city police and the mother of the victim. The extent of the gap was revealed by Mrs. Coar as she told a reporter that, 'For three years

I have suffered emotional anguish because of an incompetent police investigation and anger by the district attorney over my interference in the case. I just want to see justice done and it is his duty to provide justice.' Let there be no more of this <u>kind</u> of treatment of family members of crime victims! Police and prosecutors are as prone to error as any other human beings. When a mistake is made and someone with a personal interest in the outcome of an investigation offers help or criticism, justice is best served by acknowledging outside assistance. That course, unfortunately, was not followed soon enough in the investigation in the death of Anne Coar Hodgins."

As the press began looking deeper into the case, their shock at the bungling investigation became readily apparent. Their next piece on the case was entitled "A Disaster."

"The Hodgins' investigation was a disaster from the start. "I think we did a reasonably good job in the Genova investigation," said one city detective. "But the Hodgins case, my God, it was terrible!" How terrible? Consider some of the facts that recently surfaced. The day after the shooting, Hodgins was given a gunpowder particle detection test to determine if he had recently handled a gun. The test of his hands showed a strong positive reaction. A test of Mrs. Hodgins' left hand showed a weak positive reaction. The gunpowder test given Anne and Tom Hodgins proves little, because it was outdated three years ago. A more superior test, the neutron activation test, should have been given the couple. It could have been given because it was available. No one knows

why it wasn't. Then, there was the trouble police had finding the gun with which she was shot. The cops looked all over the apartment until her husband suggested they look under the cushion of the chair in which the seriously wounded woman was found. A .38–caliber derringer was found stuck between the cushion and one arm of the chair. Instead of gently handling the weapon in order to protect fingerprints on it, an officer grabbed the gun, damaging the prints and the possibility of detecting if the weapon's handle had been wiped clean. There's other circumstantial evidence detectives overlooked in the case and it's hard to believe professionals supposedly dedicated to the protection of the public can be so clumsy when it comes to investigating a possible murder."

I was privy to some of the mistakes made in the investigation, but others came as a complete surprise, greatly upsetting me. I worried that the botched investigation would make it impossible for a jury to convict Tom. My worries only increased when the Times ran the following editorial on August 7, 1983.

"The latest development in the already bizarre investigation of the murder of Anne Coar Hodgins is almost too much to believe. A portion of the scalp of the victim, which had been in police custody at City Hall, is now missing and the subject of a search. This case has been botched from the outset. Some very basic police work that should have been done was either not done at all or was not done correctly. The gunpowder test on the hands of the victim was

outdated by modern police standards. A more superior test that could have been administered to the victim and her husband might have been much more helpful. The location of the bullet entry indicated that the victim had used her left hand, but she was right-handed. Then there was the matter of the gun police found between the cushion and arm of the chair. It was retrieved in a manner that prevented taking fingerprints from it. In addition, the victim's clothing was discarded without being tested for bloodstains. Such markings might have been helpful in determining her position when the bullet entered her head. Most of these things might never have become general knowledge had not Mrs. Coar pushed for a reopening of the probe. She hired a private investigator and he uncovered plenty of evidence indicating that this was not a suicide. Still, when she virtually forced a second autopsy to be conducted, she was told she would have to pay the cost of the second autopsy. What an incredible reaction! She should have been given a medal for public service! All those circumstances are strange enough but the latest development surpasses them all. The part of the scalp that is missing is evidence in a murder case. It could indicate many things, including the closeness of the gun when the bullet was fired. The evidence should not have been lost—this is too sloppy to comprehend! This is a case that cries out for a thorough investigation by a neutral agency of police investigative procedures. When an incident such as this come to light we wonder how many more probes are similarly botched. The public deserves to know all there is to know about this matter and it must be assured it will not happen again"

The investigation took time. Months went by, but I wasn't unhappy about that since Tom, unable to meet bail, was languishing in jail. But knowing a trial was coming was stressful, and needing to get away and clear my head, I decided that for Thanksgiving I would take Marilyn and Nancy to Disney World. While there we witnessed the Light Parade and gorgeous sunsets, but we ate gnocchi for Thanksgiving dinner, because I had a difficult time carrying on the traditions of a thirty year marriage that ended with Stan's death. The first holidays after a death are so fraught with memories that one can hardly function, and even today, because so many tragedies in my family have occurred on or around holidays, I literally hold my breath, wondering what tragedy will occur on the next one.

The girls enjoyed themselves, and we rented a car and had some hair-raising rides on the freeway from Kissimmee to Orlando, but we had a marvelous time and I truly enjoyed their enthusiasm as we tried to forget Thanksgivings past. All too soon it was time to come back and face whatever our future had in store for us.

On December 12, 1983 Assistant District Attorney William Fisher and I met in Stuart James's office in Binghamton. Fisher wanted my blessing in offering Tom a plea bargain; Tom would plead guilty to third degree manslaughter and receive a sentence of seven to ten years. As part of the plea agreement, he would also be allowed out of jail for the holidays. Knowing Tom's past history of running, I could not, and would not, agree to this.

"I think a jury would find him guilty of third degree murder with a heavier sentence," I said, "so let's take him to trial." I wanted Tom Hodgins in jail forever.

CHAPTER EIGHT

Jury selection in the Commonwealth of Pennsylvania versus Thomas Hodgins began on January 3, 1984 in the Lackawanna County Courthouse before Judge James Walsh. Standing in for the prosecution was Assistant District Attorney William Fisher, and for the defense, Attorney Lee Krause of Honesdale.

Members of my family—Cathy, Aileen, who took a leave from the Army and came up from Georgia, Kim Mangan, my niece, and as many friends who could, sat in the front seats with me. What a great comfort that was since, sitting opposite on the left side of the courtroom, were Tom's mother, Ann Nelson, accompanied by her son Jimmy, and his now-wife, Debbie. Jimmy and Debbie had since moved to California, and subpoenaed by the court to testify, they stayed for only one week before flying back home. Afterward, Ann Nelson sat alone for most of the trial, clutching her Rosary and taking notes.

Due to the heavy publicity, the choosing of a jury took two weeks. Most of the prospective jurors had already made up their minds that Tom was guilty. The jury was comprised of seven males and five females—housewives, factory workers, an executive secretary, super market cashier, credit manager, budget director and truck driver. Only one, a teacher, had more than a high school education.

When ADA William Fisher rose to his begin his opening, he

told the jury that Tom Hodgins was "desperate for money," and had taken a life insurance policy out on his wife that would be worth fifty-thousand dollars if she died accidentally. A policy which was taken out on August 8, 1980, less than a month before she was shot. Anne Hodgins was also right-handed, Fisher said, and he "would call witnesses who would testify to that."

Lee Krause insisted that Anne had committed suicide and his client had had nothing to do with her death. Tom loved his wife he told the jury, he would not hurt her. He also reminded them that "Hodgins had dropped a one-hundred thousand dollar policy on his wife because he could not afford the premiums."

The first witness called for the state was Detective William Walsh, who testified that he investigated Anne's death on September 2, 1980.

Asked what his "investigation" consisted of, Walsh answered, "I ordered the taking of the table and chair in which she was found."

Cathy's husband, Todd Green was called next. He described himself as Anne's brother-in-law and told the jury that, "I went to Anne's apartment on September second with my wife, Cathy, and her sister, Aileen, and saw blood and brain inside the lamp shade."

The shade, however, had not been taken into evidence by the police and when asked about this, Todd said he had brought it to the police after it was taken out of storage in Fortuner's warehouse, where it had been stored since October 1980.

Todd described Tom's differing stories for where he was when the gun went off as "conflicting."

"What do you mean by that?" Fisher asked.

"Well, at one point he said he was cleaning the kitchen, and later, that he was checking the children." Todd also related how Tom told him they had been "shooting up on East Mountain," and when Todd asked him when he had taught Anne how to handle a gun, Tom had answered, "Never."

"Had you ever seen your sister-in-law with a weapon?" Fisher asked.

"No," Todd said, shaking his head, "Anne hated guns and would never have one in the house."

"Mr. Green, which hand was Anne's dominant hand?"

"Her right," Todd answered firmly.

Sherry Lacone, took the stand to tell of buying Anne's car on the Saturday of her death and of Anne telling her to "keep in touch" as she departed.

"Had you know Tom or Anne previously?" Fisher asked.

"Yes," Sherry answered. "I had met Tom several years before, at the Dickson City VFW where he drank."

Glenna Laybourne glared at Tom as she took the stand and told the jury that Anne was right-handed and clumsy with her left hand. "She even joked about it," Glenna said. She described working for Tom for three months as a secretary at Electra-Sonic, and said she left because the business was failing and irate customers were calling to complain. She had decided to "get out," she said, but had trouble collecting her last paycheck.

It was clear that Glenna did not like Tom as she recalled her visit to Lackawanna State Park with Anne when she saw Tom following his wife and stalking her. Tom would "not allow Anne to go anywhere without him, was very jealous, and the last time the two had visited at her house, they had fought the entire time."

Anne was not suicidal, Glenna insisted. "She directed her anger outward, never inward. She was a strong-willed, vain woman, who hated guns"

Prudential Life Insurance agent, James Hicks, told the jury about writing life insurance policies for both Anne and Tom and how Anne had called him to change the amounts and beneficiary on a 1976 twenty-five thousand dollar policy from Michael Revak, to Cathy Green.

"Did she ask you to make any other changes?" Fisher asked.

"Yes," Hicks replied, "She also asked that I decrease the amounts on the present two policies for one-hundred thousand dollars, which I did." Only the first premium had been paid on that policy so it lapsed in October. On September 16, 1980, Hicks continued, at a meeting at Ann Nelson's home in Jermyn, with Cathy and Tom, Tom applied for the insurance proceeds, insisting Anne's death was "accidental" and he would "hire a pathologist to prove it."

"Did the policy on Anne have a suicide clause?"

"It did," Hick's answered. "The policy would not pay out for suicide during the first two years."

"Did Tom Hodgins know this?" Fisher asked.

"Objection," Krause called.

"Sustained."

"Was the policy ever paid to Mr. Hodgins?"

"No it was not."

Lucille Haines Smith took the stand and told of how she and Tom had lived together despite Tom still being married to his wife Karen. Lucille had two children at the time, and subsequently had a set of twins with Tom. Karen's son, Sean was Tom's child and when Karen and Sean moved to Dundaff, Pennsylvania, Tom, Lucille and their four children moved in with her.

"Was Tom still married to Karen at this time?" Fisher asked.

"Yes," Lucille answered.

"And how long did you and Tom and your four children live with Karen and Sean?"

"For four months, until Karen took Sean and went back to Ohio."

After that, Lucille continued, she and Tom had rented an apartment in Jermyn where they lived until Tom met Anne and moved in with her in August of 1979. After Anne's death, Lucille continued, Tom came to visit her and she had asked him what had happened.

"What did Tom tell you?"

"He said he was downstairs smoking a cigarette when he heard the gun go off."

"Did you ever know Tom Hodgins to have a gun?"

"Yes," Lucille said, "Tom had a gun which he kept in his car."

"Did Tom say anything about insurance at that time?"

"Yes, he said there was a big insurance policy and that he would buy clothes for the kids when he collected on it."

"Mrs. Smith, were you and Tom Hodgins ever married?"

"No."

"What surname do your children go by?"

"Hodgins."

Fisher raised his eyebrows. "All of them, or just the twins?"

"All of them," Lucille said, "They're Tom's children."

It was an unusual answer. *Were* all of Lucille's children Toms? If so, he must have been having an affair with her for much longer than his wife, Karen, or anyone else knew. It certainly wouldn't have surprised me.

***

Anne's sister, Cathy cried softly when she told the jury that she had spoken to Anne by phone on August 23, 1980, at which time Anne invited her and Todd to "join us for dinner for Mom and Dad's anniversary next week." Anne had also mentioned looking into getting a VA loan so she and Tom could buy a house.

"How did Anne sound?" Fisher asked.

"She was happy about the sale of her car," Cathy replied, "but also worried because they were strapped for cash and Amy needed clothes for school."

Cathy described going to Anne's house on September 2 with

her sister Aileen, when they observed dirty dishes in the sink and hardly any food in the refrigerator. "We also saw blood spatter inside the lampshade, and crumpled-up bloody papers scattered on the floor." She recalled how she scrubbed the blood off the table, so "Tom wouldn't see it."

"You were the beneficiary on Anne's life insurance policy?" Fisher asked.

"Yes," Cathy replied.

"Can you tell the jury what became of those proceeds?"

Cathy recalled how she had paid the funeral expenses then paid twenty-three hundred dollars to customers from Electra-Sonic whose money Tom had taken but whose furnaces he never installed. She then gave $1000 to each of her siblings and parents and placed the remainder in trust for Anne's daughter, Amy.

Fisher then called two of Tom's Electra-Sonic customers; Frank Clark and Robert Henwood to describe how Tom had ripped them off.

Clark testified that he called Tom repeatedly, ordering him to either "hook [the furnace] up or return my money." When that didn't work, Clark filed charges against him with the Magistrate in the spring of 1980.

"Did you ever receive any compensation for your ordeal?" Fisher asked.

"Yes," Clark replied, "I received a check for nine-hundred and fifty dollars in September of 1980 after which I went to the magistrate and dropped the charges."

"Whose signature was on that check?"

"Cathy Green's."

Robert Henwood also dropped his complaint after he received a check from Cathy Green in the amount of one-thousand one-hundred and fifty-six dollars.

In the front row, I sat seething. Tom Hodgins had not only murdered my daughter, but he had persuaded Cathy to use Anne's blood money to pay for her funeral and his debts. He had also stolen what she owned when he married her, kept the four-hundred dollars Anne received from selling her car, and sold her furniture and most of her possessions.

***

I couldn't help but feel hopeful by the way the trial was progressing. Tom was coming off looking like the con-man I knew him to be, but that didn't stop me from worrying.

The prosecution's next witness was Tom's friend, Jerry Warnero. Warnero told the jury how he had been thrown from his motorcycle after an accident and was bleeding heavily when Tom came on the scene.

"He saved my life by applying a tourniquet," Warnero said.

Warnero said he wanted to thank Tom for his heroics that day and that Tom later showed him a gun in a catalog which Warnero agreed to purchase for him out of gratitude.

"Mr. Warnero, were you with Tom Hodgins on August 11, 1980?"

"I was," Warnero answered. He had been present when Tom purchased a gun from Al Messina that day.

"Did you give Tom anything that day?"

"Yes, I gave Tom two bullets; rounded, 38 special, hollow point, 6 grain unique powder standard load."

"And did you make any adjustments to Mr. Hodgin's new weapon?"

Again, Warnero answered in the affirmative. He had taken the gun and after jewelling and reducing the trigger pull weight, he gave the gun back to Tom.

"Is this the weapon Mr. Hodgins purchased that day?" Fisher asked, offering his witness the .38 Derringer.

Warnero peered at the gun and nodded. "Yes, that's the gun."

"And is this one of the bullets you gave him?"

Again, Warnero looked closely at the ammunition and admitted that it was.

"And what was your reason for adjusting the trigger on this weapon?"

"Tom told me Anne would be shooting the gun and asked me to reduce the pull on the trigger for her."

Fisher next began calling his "expert" witnesses.

Dale Allen of the Scranton Police Lab, described the .38 bullet used in the Derringer as "designed to mushroom as it separates." He had test fired the gun in a tank of water, noted the land and groove markings on the bullets, and then conducted a trigger-pull test.

"What were the results of those tests," Fisher asked.

"The trigger had a seven pound, six ounce pull. It was not a hair trigger. I also conducted some testing whereby I cocked the hammer and then dropped the weapon from several different heights to see if I could get it to accidentally discharge."

"And did you?"

"No," Allen said, shaking his head. "It went to half-cock, but I could not get it to accidentally fire."

"Detective Allen, what is this type of weapon normally used for?"

"Home defense."

"What about target shooting?"

"Not typically."

"How about hunting?"

Allen shrugged. "Yes, it could be used for hunting."

"Does the gun have a recoil?"

"It does."

"Would the gun require two hands to fire?"

"No, it would not."

Lieutenant Paul of the Philadelphia Police Lab had also test-fired the .38 with the same type of bullets that had killed Anne; a 6 grain unique gunpowder.

"What did those tests show, Lieutenant?" Fisher asked.

"When fired up to twelve inches, the object showed stippling—small black specks—around the wound with minute traces of soot, and carbon, as well as un-burnt traces of gunpowder and residue. Up to four inches, considerable scorching and stippling occurred with the muzzle flash.

"What is this gun typically used for?"

"For self-protection—defense—and to kill."

"Could you tell us what occurs when someone is shot with this weapon."

Turning towards the jury, Paul said that dense stippling would result from a close entry wound, while minimal tattooing would occurred if the gun were fired about eight inches from the target. The weapon would create a hole with at least a one and a half to one and three quarter inch radius. If the weapon was in close proximity, it would create sixteen-thousand pounds of pressure as it entered the wound canal and the gases would back up, causing a satellite tear with radiating cracks. If the weapon were fired about an inch away from the target, scorching would be found. At four inches away, some of the gunpowder, carbon, nitrates, and un-burnt powder would all enter into the wound canal, and one would find burnt hair and stippling. At eight to twelve inches it would create a sparse pattern of nitrates with no discernible pattern.

"Lieutenant, do you know if there was any stippling found around Mrs. Hodgins wound?"

"I don't believe there was."

"Would you then consider this a close entry wound or not?"

"I would have to say it was not a close entry wound."

As Krause rose to cross-examine the witness he asked, "Lieutenant Paul, you stated that dense stippling would result from a close entry wound, but I'm wondering, would hair have any effect on that?"

"Yes," Paul acknowledged, "Hair could create a filtering, especially dense hair." (Which of course, Anne, with her abundance of thick, full hair, had.)

"You also noted that the weapon would create a hole with at least a one and a half to one and three quarter inch radius, but again, would hair affect that?"

"The wound could diminish rapidly because of hair closer than eight inches."

"Thank you Lieutenant."

The next witness to take the stand would describe, perhaps, the biggest blunder in the entire investigation.

George Serman, who was with the Wyoming County Police Lab, and who had had only fifteen hours of case training, told the jury that he accepted from Detective Hart the incised wound from Anne's head. The scalp and hair from both the left and right side of her head had been removed to preserve the entry and exit wounds.

"What did you do with this evidence?" Fisher asked.

"I locked it in the evidence room until I could study it."

"And did you study it?"

"I did, and I found the wound clean, with no gunpowder and charring."

"And did you do any analysis on the wound?"

Serman looked uncomfortable as he shook his head, no.

"And why not?" Fisher asked.

"The hair had the results of putrefaction, and was therefore unusable for analysis."

Incredibly, Anne's head wound had been kept in a refrigerator, but, due to a power failure, had begun to decay and so was useless for testing.

"What did you do with the evidence after that?"

"I returned the evidence to Detective Hart on October thirty-first, and I assume it was returned to locked storage."

Stan Striefsky, one of the first emergency medical technicians on the scene the night Anne was shot, testified that he and his partner, Don Snyder had arrived at the house at 3:15 a.m.

"What did you observe upon entering the house?"

"We saw Anne in the recliner, with her arms hanging over the arm rests and one foot off the footrest."

"Was she reclined in the chair?"

"No, sir."

"Was she breathing?"

"No, she was not breathing, but she did have a pulse. We intubated her and began an intravenous line through which we gave her Valium to prevent convulsions."

"Did you see a weapon?"

"No," the witness answered, shaking his head, "No weapon, but Don spotted the bullet with a copper jacket on the floor to the right of the chair."

"Was there a table near the chair?"

"There was. The table was located to the left of the chair and had a lamp on it. I asked Mr. Hodgins to remove the lampshade so that I would have more light to work".

"Can you describe for the jury the wound Anne Hodgins received?"

"The bullet had entered above the left ear and exited behind the right."

When Krause rose to cross-examine, he wasted no time. "So Mr. Hodgins was there while you worked on his wife?"

"Yes, he was there."

"Was he crying?"

The witness looked thoughtful for a moment. "I don't recall that he was crying."

"Did he appear upset?"

"Yes, he did."

On that note, Judge Walsh adjourned court for the day.

***

Listening to the details of my daughter's death was gut-wrenching, but I continued to tell myself that it would all be worth it in the end. I had no doubt that soon I would hear the jury speak that one word; "guilty."

The first witness to take the stand the next morning was Patrolman Virgil Argenta, the first policeman on the scene.

"Officer," Fisher began, "Did you ask Mr. Hodgins what had

happened"

"I did," Argenta said, "And he told me he was downstairs having a smoke when he heard a bang. I asked him about any weapons he owned and he said that he kept a loaded Derringer in his office."

"Did you see a weapon at the scene?"

"No, I did not, and I searched for one. After a bit, Mr. Hodgins told me to look in the chair and I did so, finally finding it down in the chair, between the left side of the cushion and the left arm."

How could the weapon have ended up there, I wondered?

"What did you do with the weapon once you retrieved it?" Fisher continued.

"I handed it to Detective Borgia, who placed it in a handkerchief."

"What was Mr. Hodgins doing? What was his demeanor?"

"Mr. Hodgins kept asking where his wife's purse was. Over and over again he asked about her purse. He finally found it on a chair on the front porch where she said she had been sitting.
I recall his demeanor as matter-of-fact."

"Matter of fact? Explain what you mean by that."

"He didn't seem frantic, and I remember him casually shaking hands with Officer Al Sames when he arrived, and asking him 'How are you?'"

Krause sounded annoyed as he asked the witness, "You're saying the defendant's behavior was suspicious?"

"It wasn't what I expected." Argenta said.

"People react to stressful situations differently, don't they?"

"Yes, that's true," the witness admitted.

Krause, having made his point, should have stopped right there but he didn't. "You considered my client's behavior suspicious, didn't you?"

"He wasn't acting like I'd expect a husband to act if his wife just shot herself."

"But, you didn't note that in any report, did you officer?"

"No, but it did prompt me to call the hospital and tell the nurse to bag the victim's hands since no one had bothered to do that."

Even angrier now, Krause asked Argenta how he retrieved the gun from inside the chair.

"With a pen, inside the barrel."

Stalking back to the defense table, the attorney picked up a sheet of paper and approached the witness. Handing it to him, he asked Argenta, "Is this a statement you wrote?"

The officer glanced at the paper and nodded. "Yes, it is."

"Doesn't it say on there that you retrieved the gun by its trigger guard?"

"Yes, it does. But that was a mistake. I retrieved it with a pen inside the barrel."

"Oh, I see, that was a mistake," Krause said sarcastically. "I have nothing further for this witness."

Although Tom had told Officer Argenta that he was "downstairs having a smoke when he heard the gun go off, he told

Detective Clem Borgia something else entirely. Borgia told the jury that Tom told him that he and Anne had been at his brother's house earlier that evening, and 'When we came home, Anne found a letter on the steps and became upset. The letter was apparently from their landlord telling them their offer on the house had been rejected. Tom said Anne then went inside and afterward I heard a shot.'"

"Detective," Fisher asked, "Did you see a weapon at the scene?"

"Not at first. In fact, it took the officers forty-five minutes to find it down in the chair."

"What was Mr. Hodgins' demeanor at the time?"

"He seemed nervous and edgy."

"Do you recall anything else about Mr. Hodgins from that night?"

"Well, when Detective Hart arrived, the police photographer, I heard Mr. Hodgins tell him that he was down checking the children when he heard the shot fired."

"Objection, hearsay," Krause shouted, jumping to his feet.

"Sustained," Judge Walsh replied. "The jury will disregard that last statement."

On cross, Krause asked Borgia how much involvement he had in the case.

"I made my report after 8:00 a.m. and had no more involvement in the case after that." Sergeant Clem Ross stated that Tom had also told him that he was "down the hall checking the children when he heard the shot," but Tom had also added that he and Anne had been arguing. "Mr. Hodgins told me that he and Anne went to Jermyn to Tom's brother's house where they were out shooting a gun, and that when they came home, Anne told him to leave.' I asked Mr. Hodgins which hand was his wife's dominant hand and he said 'her right,' but quickly added, 'She could shoot with either hand.'"

"Did you also interview Amy Kalasinsky, Anne's daughter by a previous marriage?" Fisher asked.

"I did," Ross answered. "I asked her if her father came in to check on her and Amy said that Mr. Hodgins came into her room and said, 'your mother has shot herself—don't leave your room.' I then asked her how he seemed, and she replied, 'nervous and edgy.'"

"Did Amy give you a description of what had occurred that day?"

"She told me that she didn't think Tom and her mother were out shooting that afternoon because her mother had found the gun in the glove compartment of the car when they went to the Carbondale picnic that night, and had asked Tom, 'What do you have a gun for?' Amy had also told Officer Ross that she "Heard a door slam and then a shot," after which Tom came into her room.

***

The majority of the next day's testimony would be taken up by medical personnel.

Dr. Platt, the neurosurgeon, testified that Anne had, "A left temporal-parietal entrance wound and an exit wound below the right ear. The left wound was clean, and shaved by me. I saw no dark areas, no marking, and no powder burns."

"Was Mrs. Hodgins conscious?" Fisher asked.

"No, she was unconscious and unable to breath without the respirator. I noted no movement to her extremities. The bullet had advanced to the brainstem—which controls involuntary function, such as breathing and movements of face and eyes—as well as through the cerebral cortex"

"Could the victim have moved after sustaining this wound?"

"No."

"Was there any response to painful stimuli?"

"No."

Looking confused, Fisher asked the doctor why Anne was put on life support if her injuries could not sustain life."

"For organ donation," Dr. Platt said simply.

Lackawanna County Coroner, William Sweeney testified that he listed Anne's cause of death on September 4, 1980 as "pending," and changed it to "homicide" on August 29, 1983 following the second autopsy conducted on the body.

When Dr. Dominick DeMaio, the pathologist who performed the original autopsy took the stand, he stated that the angle of the bullet was downward and from left to right at a forty-five degree angle. "The wound indicated neither explosion nor contact effect, and, I could not rule her death a homicide. I had come to no conclusion at that time, pending further police investigation."

DeMaio's testimony seemed odd. If the wound was a non-contact wound, that would mean that Anne had not only used her non-dominant hand to fire the weapon, but she had held it in an unnatural position, above—but away from—her head and pointing downwards. In trying to reconstruct it myself, I found that it is not only an unnatural position, but an uncomfortable, and nearly impossible one.

DeMaio continued by saying that "The wound had been excised by me and sent to the State Police Laboratory," but the hair had been disturbed and cleansed by the hospital personnel. "There was a large abundance of hair on the head," and although he had sent the excised wound to the State Lab for testing, he never received any results.

DeMaio was a godsend for the defense. "So doctor, you could not rule out suicide in Mrs. Hodgin's death, could you?"

"No. I could not."

What about after the second autopsy?"

"I still could not, with certainty, rule out suicide"

Dr. Halbert Fillinger had no uncertainties. He told the jury that during Anne's second autopsy on March 2, 1983, he found "A penetrating wound three and one-half inches above the left ear, with an exit wound one half-inch below the right ear." He also saw no gunpowder residue, indicating that this was a non-contact wound and the weapon was not in close range of the skull when the shot was fired. "I can say, with reasonable certainty, that this was not a self- inflicted injury"

Dr. Michael Baden, the renowned forensic pathologist, agreed with his colleague. He told the jury that although "the skin about the entrance wound was absent, the bullet went through the skull bone and he found no evidence of powder or soot on the bone." The trajectory of the bullet—from left to right, downward and to the back—indicated that this "was not a contact wound, but a single gunshot wound with a probable distance beyond twelve to eighteen inches."

Twelve to eighteen inches? If the shot had been fired from twelve to eighteen inches away, then it was an absolute impossibility that Anne had shot herself.

"Doctor," Prosecutor Fisher asked, "Was there any indication of gun powder residue on or near Mrs. Hodgin's wound?

"No," Baden answered. "When a gun is fired, there are flames, smoke, granules, and slivers of metal and they were not present."

Fisher then threw out a hypothetical question. "Doctor, assuming the victim is found in a chair and the head is on the right side and the gun is found in the chair, and no high velocity blood spatter is found on the chair, and no burning or singeing of the victim's hair is seen by the physician, what would be your opinion?"

"That death occurred from a gunshot wound, with the manner of death being a homicide."

"And doctor, how much experience have you had with victim's being killed by gunshot?"

"I've conducted over fifteen-thousand autopsies, of which approximately four-hundred *per year* are gunshot wounds."

"Thank you doctor."

Lee Krause first asked Dr. Baden if Anne's death could have been a suicide.

"This wound was not consistent with suicide," Baden said, going on to explain. "Self-inflicted wounds have characteristics on the side of the dominant hand—in other words, suicides always use their dominant hand. Additionally, self-inflicted wounds are always in contact with the skin, and in this case, neither was true. Here we have a distant wound, and the victim using her left hand, which is inconsistent with suicide."

Quickly moving away from that topic, Krause asked who brought the doctor into the case.

"Robert Jennings and Stuart James, but I was contacted by the District Attorney in March of 1983, and I ultimately submitted my report to him."

"Doctor, what about the victim's state of mind? Did you consider it in this case?"

"No," Baden said, shaking his head, "Because it was atypical of suicide. From my findings, it would have been possible for Mrs. Hodgin's hand to reach only eight to ten inches, and there was no powder in the bone on re-autopsy. Her dominant hand was not used, and she was not shot where she was found. If the head were bent to the left, the wound would have been more horizontal."

Wisely, Krause let Dr. Baden go after that.

Stuart James, the investigator I had first contacted, took the stand next, and told the jury that he had done a reconstruction of the crime. "Using the chair, table, lamp and shade, I looked for bullet holes, particles of hair, scorching, gunpowder residue, and anything else pertinent to a crime scene. I found no bullet holes and no hair, and swabbing for blood on the right side of the chair was negative."

Swabbing for blood on the right side of the chair was negative? How could that be if Tom were telling the truth? Anne had supposedly shot herself while reclining in the chair, with her head turned to the right. The bullet had exited the below her right ear. Blood had been found on the back, and left side of the chair, but none on the right side. How could that be?

"And did you reach any conclusion from these discoveries?" Fisher continued.

"I did," James answered. "I concluded that the chair would have to have been upright if she were sitting when she was shot, in order for the blood to continue down the back of the chair because the nature of the upholstery of the chair was non-absorbent. The drip pattern of the blood was directed down and around the left shoulder which was outlined in blood. A large quantity of blood had also dripped onto the floor."

"What does all this mean?"

"It means that the victim bled in close contact with the chair, and that the bleeding occurred while the chair was in an upright position and not reclined as the emergency medical technicians found her."

"And this indicated. . . ?

"It indicated that the body had been moved from the position in which it was found. Not a single drop of blood was noted where she was resting against the chair, which shows the body had been moved."

"Did you look for blood spatter or transfer patterns?"

"I did, and I found numerous spots encircled inside the lampshade which tested positive for blood. Their size indicated high velocity blood spatter, and the lampshade had a waxy material consistent with human origin.

"And what did that tell you?"

"Well, since high velocity spatter travels in a straight line, and there was no blood spatter inside the shade, I again concluded that the spatter occurred when the chair was upright."

"Did you also examine the gun?"

"I did, and I found no trace of blood as such on the tip of the muzzle."

On cross, Krause asked if the blood on the lampshade could have been caused by the emergency medical technicians.

"Only if picked straight up. It's my conclusion that the victim was neither sitting nor standing in front of the chair [when she was shot] and that the scene was altered by another person."

Chemist William Edwards of Sirchie Labs in Raleigh, North Carolina next took the stand to testify about the gunshot residue kit from Anne's hands. "If one fires a weapon," Edwards told the jury, "residue is deposited on their hands." In order to determine if nitrites are present, the police swab the person's hands and transfer the swabs to blotter paper. Afterward, a solution is sprayed on the paper which will turn pink if nitrites are detected.

"Doctor, can you conclude differences in concentration on two hands, if one were positive and another tested weaker?"

"If the person fired the gun themselves, there would be a greater concentration on that person's hand. At a farther distance, there would be a less positive reaction."

"Did you find any gunshot residue on Anne's hands?"

"I found a very small trace amount on one of her hands."

"Is firing a gun the only way Mrs. Hodgins could have gotten nitrites on her hand?"

"No, some things in the household can create a positive reaction as well. Nitrites are used in hotdogs, cosmetics and other food, but the amounts are so minute they would not show a positive reaction." (Although Edwards didn't add it, there was also the possibility that if a person put up their hand to ward off an oncoming bullet, that could leave trace evidence behind as well.)

On cross, Krause asked if he had tested Tom's hands for nitrites.

"I did, and the tests were negative."

On re-direct, Fisher asked if washing a floor would remove the nitrites from someone's hands." (Tom had washed the floor before his hands were tested.)

If there was an abundant quantity of nitrites on the hands it could possibly test positive, but after four or five hours, the material would be lost, and would diminish, so I do not know if it would still be detectable."

On re-cross, Edwards was asked, "If someone shot close range, say eight to ten inches away, or moved the victim's head would that indicate rather large quantities of nitrites?"

"Yes."

Incredibly, there was a much more advanced test for gunshot residue at the time, but the Scranton Police apparently were not aware of it. When Detective Captain Roche was asked if newer powder tests were available, he replied, "I was the only one aware of them."

"Captain," Fisher asked, "Did you examine the gun?"

"Detective Hart and I did. It had a pencil in the barrel and under the microscope it had no prints at all."

Val Seymour, a prisoner at the Lackawanna County Jail told the jury that when Tom received his divorce papers from Bunny Lyons, he vowed to "fix her like I fixed the other one."

"Did Mr. Hodgins say anything else?"

"Yes," Seymour stated, he then said, "I killed her."

The prosecution's case was winding down. After calling gun

dealer, Al Messina to testify to Tom purchasing the gun that killed Anne only twenty-seven days before she was shot, Fisher put on witnesses to tell of Tom's jealousy and possessiveness towards his wife.

Estelle Doherty, Anne's hairdresser repeated for the jury how Anne confided in her that she wasn't able to go out without Tom because of his jealousy, and Janet Kalasinski, recalled the time Tom showed up at her door.

"Tell the jury what happened that day," Fisher told her.

"It was the summer of 1980," Janet said, "And Tom came to her home very upset, and told her that 'Stanley and Anne are seeing each other. They communicate at RCA,' which is where Stan was employed."

"What else did Tom tell you that day?"

"He told me, 'I have a gun, and I'm a member of the Mafia, but believe me, not as a mechanic. He also told me, 'I never hit a woman before, but she'll be the first.'"

"Can you describe Mr. Hodgin's appearance that day?"

"He had scratches on his chest, and told me Anne had inflicted them during an argument."   "Mrs. Kalasinski, why did Tom Hodgins come to visit you that day?"

"To get Stanley to stop calling Anne"

When the defense elected not to question Janet Kalasinski, Fisher turned towards the bench.

"Your Honor, the state calls Anne Coar."

From the moment I realized that Tom Hodgins had murdered my daughter, I had begun preparing myself for this day, but it was still an incredibly surreal moment to be walking to that witness stand.

District Attorney Fisher led me through the phone call from Tom's mother that night and mine and Stan's arrival at the hospital.

"When we got there, I asked where the wound was and when they told me it was on the left side, I immediately said, 'but she's right handed.' From that moment on, I knew something was wrong."

On cross, Lee Krause asked me about Anne's mental state. "Didn't you tell Detective Hart that Anne was depressed? Didn't you tell him that she had taken pills? (Apparently in a suicide attempt.)

"I never said Anne took pills," I answered, shaking my head vehemently. "Anne never, never took pills. Detective Hart kept pressing me to tell him of her depression and I said, 'She was taking us out for our wedding anniversary that day—I can't believe she'd do something like this.' I also told him, "I talked to her a week before, when she invited us out to dinner for our anniversary and my son's birthday."

"But didn't you tell him she was depressed?"

"I told him, 'She's been going off the deep end because of the business failure, but I did not say she had taken pills to commit suicide. Tom was the only person who said Anne had taken pills."

When I finally stepped down from the witness chair, District Attorney Fisher turned once more to Judge Walsh and said, "Your Honor, the Commonwealth rests."

CHAPTER NINE

Debbie Hodgins, Tom's sister-in-law was the first witness called by the defense. She told the jury that "Tommy and Jimmy" had fired a muzzle loader at 5:30 that afternoon before going to the Mayfield picnic, and then to Pioneer Days in Carbondale. Afterward, Debbie said they all went to her and Jimmy's apartment and played cards.

"How did you hear about Anne's shooting?" Krause asked.

"Early on the morning of August 31, my Aunt Marion came to the house and called up the stairs to come to the hospital."

James "Jimmy" Hodgins testified that his brother fired both the Derringer pistol—which was used to shoot Anne—and a muzzle-loading handgun nine hours before Anne was killed.

"What did you do that evening?" Krause asked.

Jimmy described how he and his wife, Debbie, and Tom and Anne went to a pair of community picnics, after which, they played cards at his Jermyn home until about midnight.

"Did anything happen during the card game?"

"Yes, while we were playing the card game Uno, Anne unjustly accused me of cheating. She went to the bathroom and when she returned, her spirits were uplifted."

In the gallery I felt myself bristle. What was Jimmy trying to say? That Anne had gone in the bathroom and "used" something—perhaps a pill—to "uplift" her spirits?

"Later," Jimmy continued, "Anne became upset and threw a

chair at Tom after finding a note that indicated her husband had taken a day off of work. Then she stormed out of the house after screaming at Tom."

Fisher's demeanor was accusatory as he began his cross.

"Didn't you tell the police in October, 1980 that on August 30, 1980 you had to use two hands to fire the Derringer because the "kick" or "jolt" forced both your hands up in the air?"

"No," Jimmy said, shaking his head. "I told them that on an earlier occasion I had to use two fingers because it was difficult to squeeze the trigger. On August 30, 1980 I could easily discharge the weapon with one hand."

"Mr. Hodgins, where did you brother keep the gun?"

"In the glove compartment of the car."

"Tell me how you learned about Anne's shooting."

Jimmy related that after Anne and Tom had gone home, he and Debbie went to bed. "We were sleeping and Debbie was awakened by Aunt Marion blowing her car horn. We went downstairs and Aunt Marion told us Anne shot herself so we went back upstairs, got dressed and left for the hospital."

"What was your brother like at the hospital?"

"Tom was upset."

"What was he wearing?"

"A shirt I gave him."

"Did you ever go back to Tom's house after the shooting?"

"I went to the apartment on September 2, and noticed blood

inside the lampshade."

Brian Cali, who had been employed as an attorney for the Electra-Sonic business told the jury that the company was initially formed to manufacture heating units and listed Tom as president and Anne as secretary-treasurer.

"Was the business successful?" Krause asked.

"It began well," Cali answered. "In fact, there were more units sold than manufactured."

"Were there problems?"

"There were a number of consumer complaints."

"What happened to Electra-Sonic?"

"It closed in the fall of 1980, at which time I gave Tom expert advice on bankruptcy code Chapter Seven. I also advised him to liquidate the company and pay back the complainants on an installment plan."

"Did Mr. Hodgins have the money to do that?"

"No, so I advised him to get a bank loan to do so."

"And were the complainants eventually paid back in full?"

"Yes, sir, they were."

Krause paused for a moment, and then asked, "Mr. Cali, who kept the books at Electra-Sonic?"

"Anne Hodgins."

"And did you have access to those books or the business procedure?"

"No sir, I did not."

This line of questioning infuriated me. Were they trying to

make Anne out to be the thief and not Tom?

On cross, Fisher asked Cali to tell the jury where Tom got the money to pay back his disgruntled clients.

"In a meeting with Tom and Cathy Green after Anne's death, Cathy took out a bank loan using the insurance proceeds as collateral."

"So Anne's sister paid off the complainants?"

"Yes, sir."

"Not Tom Hodgins?"

"No, sir."

"How many complainants were there, Mr. Cali?"

"I was only aware of two unhappy clients."

"When did you become aware of complaints with the company?"

"In November of 1979."

"November of 1979? Less than two months after Anne began working there?"

"Yes."

"Electra-Sonic was Tom's business wasn't it? He made all the decisions, didn't he?"

"Anne had been involved in discussions [with the business.]"

"Wasn't Anne concerned about what was happening with the business?"

"Yes."

"And wasn't it Tom Hodgins who signed those contracts?'

"Tom signed the contracts, but in some instances both of them signed, and both would collect down payments."

***

The defense put on their own expert pathologist, Dr. Dimitri Constantopoulos from Allentown who told the jury that after examining the physical evidence and the gun, he believed that "this was initially a suicide."

"What led you to that belief doctor?" Krause asked.

"I took into consideration the supposed mood of the victim and her increasing irritability."

"And what is your experience in determining whether a person is the victim of suicide or homicide?"

"I've performed approximately nine-thousand autopsies to determine if they were suicides or homicides"

"And can you state that this is a homicide?"

"I cannot, with reasonable certainty, say that this is a homicide."

"Thank you, doctor."

As Fisher rose to begin his cross, he held Doctor Constantopoulos' report in his hand.

"Doctor, your words on this report are 'suggested of suicide,' what do you mean by that?

"This was a suggested suicide because her husband stated he was not in the room, and on the day of her death she was extremely irritable and possibly depressed. Depression often leads to suicide."

"So you based your opinion on what her husband had to say?"

"No, I took into consideration the victim's mood and irritability."

"The description of which came from her husband," Fisher said, sounding incredulous. When the doctor didn't respond, the prosecutor continued. "Did you also take into consideration that the victim was right-handed?"

"Yes, and although the tendency is to use the dominant hand, ten percent of suicides do not."

Frowning, Fisher asked, "Doctor, did you even bother to read the reports of Dr.'s. Baden, Fillinger and DeMaio?"

"Yes, I read them."

"What about their failure to find tattooing around the wound, and no evidence that this was a close contact wound?"

"I still cannot say that this is a homicide. The original pathologist should have done an exam of the entry wound at the time of its excision. I would prefer not to rely on the physician's observation in the hospital. With the passage of time, the wound area gone, and the brain and dura removed, it would make it less likely to see powder."

"Can you explain the blood spatter in the lampshade?"

"It was spatter from the wound."

"What about the lack of bloodstaining to suggest she was reclining in the chair when she was shot?"

Constantopoulos admitted that the body had probably been

moved, but he also thought "the very thick hair blocked blood."

Trying to get his point across, Fisher asked why anyone would move the body of a suicide victim.

The doctor shrugged slightly. "Lieutenant Paul should have tested the hair to determine if there was singeing. Proper preservation of the scene prior to autopsy was not optimal."

Indeed, it was not.

Suddenly, Fisher changed the subject. "Where are guns typically found in suicides?"

"They're usually found still in the hand." And then acknowledging for the first time that there might be a problem here, the doctor added, "The gun in the chair is inconsistent of self-infliction."

"Doctor, are you honestly saying that this was a suicide?"

Constantopoulos remained silent for a moment and it appeared he might concede to the prosecution's theory. To a point, his answer did. "With reasonable medical certainty, I cannot state that it was either suicide or homicide."

Officer Al Sames, with the Scranton Police, took the stand next. He recalled receiving a call to report to a shooting at 606 Clay Avenue in the early morning hours of August 31, 1980.

"On my arrival, Anne was on the floor, being treated by the emergency medical technicians. I saw Tom—I knew him—and I either shook, or grabbed his hand. I don't know which."

"Did you see any blood?" Krause asked.

"I observed no blood."

Later, Sames continued, he questioned Tom at Police Headquarters and Anne's parents at the hospital. He was scheduled to be off duty at 3:00 a.m. and since it was past that time, he left Detectives Borgia and Clem Ross at the hospital to continue the investigation.

On cross, Fisher asked, "What is a policeman's job at a crime scene?"

"To take over the scene, save and examine the situation, collect evidence, then make a report."

"Did you make a report that night?"

"No, I had nothing to do with the report. Borgia wrote it."

"Did you take notes?"

"No."

"Are you aware of [the police] preserving evidence?"

"Yes"

"Did you take notes or a report on evidence at the scene?"

"No, sir, I did not."

When Tom's mother, Ann Nelson took the stand and began testifying, I felt my blood pressure rise.

Ann said that Tom called her "upset and excited" at 3:30 a.m. and told her to 'come down.' "I was the first to arrive at the hospital," Ann said, "Tom arrived forty-five minutes later, followed by Mr. and Mrs. Coar, who went into the trauma room."

Krause was about to ask her another question when Ann blurted out, "Mrs. Coar knew Anne had problems, but she didn't think she'd do this."

"What was Tom's demeanor in the hospital?"

"Tom was crying and holding his head in his hands."

"Mrs. Nelson, had you ever known Anne to use her left hand for things?"

"Oh, yes," Ann nodded vigorously, "she came to my house several times and I recall her using her left hand when being served lunch, cold soda or tea."

"Did you ever ask your son what occurred that night?"

"Yes, after they pulled the plug on September 1, Tom came home with me and I asked him what happened? He told me 'Anne wanted me to stop smoking, and while smoking outside, I heard a noise and went up to investigate.'"

In discussing the meeting at her home with Tom and Anne's sister, Cathy, concerning the insurance policy, Ann claimed the policy was on Anne's rings. "The nurse at Anne's bedside gave me Anne's rings and the following Sunday I gave them back to Tom."

Tom's shirt had been taken by the police and now Krause pulled a shirt from a plastic bag and held it up. "Is this the shirt Tom was wearing that night?"

"Yes, it is."

The shirt was clean, with no bloodstains upon it.

On cross, Fisher asked Ann Nelson if Tom had two of those shirts.

"No," Ann answered, "He only has the one."

I knew Tom's mother was lying. For Christmas, 1979, I had

purchased my son-in-law Todd, that exact shirt. Tom had really admired it, so later, I purchased for him the same shirt as well. Unbeknownst to me, Anne did the same thing; she went out and bought Tom the exact same shirt. Therefore, I knew Tom had two of those shirts and I knew his mother was lying. Why? Where was the other shirt? I figured it was long gone; discarded because it was covered with blood after Tom shot my daughter.

Tom's aunt, Marion Williams took the stand to corroborate Ann Nelson's testimony. In February, 1980 Anne visited her in her home where "she drank tea and cut her ham with her left hand."

Art Evans was another inmate at the Lackawanna County Jail, but his testimony was decidedly different from that of Val Seymour. Evans told the jury that he didn't know Tom very well, but, "I was on Clay Avenue around 2:30 or 3:00 a.m. on August thirty-first and saw Tom smoking and putting boxes in a brown and white Cadillac. I walked towards him, but then I heard a bang and kept walking.

On cross, Fisher asked Evans what Tom did when he heard the bang.

"He ran towards the house."

"But you just kept walking? You weren't concerned?"

"I thought the bang was a backfire."

"What were you doing on Clay Avenue so late at night?"

Evans claimed that he was "hitchhiking up Clay Avenue to Dunmore after drinking at O'Toole's Bar, because there's very little traffic on Clay."

Why would he be hitchhiking in a place where there was little traffic, I wondered?

"Were you inebriated at the time?" Fisher asked.

"I was zonked," Evans admitted.

"How can you be so certain of the date this incident took place?"

"I always go drinking on a holiday."

"How did you happen to come forward with this information?"

"Me and Tom discussed it while we were prisoners in the jail in 1983. Tom told me to talk to Mr. Krause about me having seen him early on the morning of the shooting."

"Are you gaining anything by testifying here today, Mr. Evans?"

"No," the witness answered, shaking his head.

Anne's ex-husband, Stanley Kalasinski, took the stand and stated, "I married Anne in 1971, and we were divorced in 1973. There were lots of arguments."

"Mr. Kalasinski, you remarried after your divorce from Anne, correct?"

"Yes, I married my wife, Janet in April of 1978."

"And did anything occur at your wedding regarding Anne?"

"Yes, she followed my new wife down the aisle dressed in black."

On cross, Fisher asked, "Did you ever have occasion to talk to

Anne?"

"Yes, on issues of child support, and picking Amy up to spend time with me and Janet." "How did Anne react in arguments?"

"She would shout, not go off and sulk."

I was upset when Stan testified for the defense, but it broke my heart to see who their next witness was.

"Call Amy Kalasinski," Krause boomed.

Anne's daughter looked frightened as she walked stiffly to the witness chair.

"Amy, did your mom have a bad temper?" Krause asked gently.

My mom's temper was not too good," Amy said, breaking into tears.

"Did you mom ever hit you?"

"Yes," Amy said, recalling that her mom had "once blackened my eyes because I spit out my medicine and she slapped me and my lips were cut."

On cross, District Attorney Fisher asked her if she remembered what happened the night her mother was shot.

"There was an argument between Mom and Tom. Doors were banging and then there was quiet and then I heard a bang." There was another period of silence after that, Amy continued, before Tom came into her bedroom and told her "Your mother has just shot herself. Stay in your room."

"Amy, did you like Tom?

"Yes, we got along good."

"Did Tom take your side in arguments with your mother?"

"I'm not sure. I don't remember."

It was Detective Al Sames who initially interviewed Amy on the night of the shooting, and now Krause recalled him to the stand.

"Detective, what do your notes say regarding what Amy told you on the night Anne Hodgins was shot?"

"In my report, I have the child quoted as saying she heard a door slam and then heard someone—she took it to be the defendant—run in the house from outside. My report also notes that the child later changed the sound of the "door slam" to sound of a "shot.""

On cross, Fisher brought out that Amy had told Sames many other things about her mother, Tom, and the night of the shooting, but the jury would never hear about them because the officer never listed them on his report. "I didn't think they were pertinent," Sames said.

"Perhaps some of those other things Amy said might be listed in your notes, Officer," Fisher said sarcastically, knowing that Sames had long ago destroyed his notes regarding his interview with Amy.

"Why would you have destroyed those notes?"

Sames shrugged. "I believed the incident to be a suicide."

"Even though the autopsy report referred to the death as suspicious?" Fisher thundered.

"Even though the autopsy report referred to the death as suspicious," Sames answered.

Krause next recalled Detective Walsh to highlight some of the police blunders in the case. Walsh testified that "The wound excised from the head of the victim is lost, as is a paper used to test for gunpowder residue on the right hand of Mr. Hodgins."

Feigning surprise, Krause asked how the police could possibly have lost such vital evidence.

"There was a power failure which caused the head wound, being preserved in a freezer, to putrefy, and it was after the power failure that the wound could not be found."

"Detective, did you have any conversations with Amy Kalasinski?"

"I did."

"And where did Amy tell you Tom was when she heard the shot?"

"She told me she couldn't remember where Tom was when she heard the shot."

When Detective Walsh stepped down, Krause turned towards the bench.

"Your Honor, call Thomas Hodgins."

Tom walked casually to the stand and took his seat, then turned and smiled at the jurors.

"Tom," Krause began, "Did you ever tell an inmate that you killed your wife?"

Tom, knowing exactly who Krause was talking about, shook his head. "I never said that to Val Seymour. Not then, not now, not ever."

"Did you kill your wife?"

"No sir, I didn't!"

"Did you shoot her in the head?"

"No."

Tom testified that he married Anne in November 1979, even though his divorce from his wife, Karen, did not become final until a few days later.

"Tom, tell the jury what you did on the afternoon of August 30, 1980."

"That afternoon, me and my brother, Jim went shooting. I shot a black powder muzzle-loader and the Derringer. Afterwards, the four of us, me, Anne, Jim and Debbie went to the Mayfield picnic and then to Pioneer Days in Carbondale. When we left there, we went back to Jimmy's house and started playing cards." He went on to describe Anne's seemingly erratic mood during the game and her anger when she discovered a note indicating he had taken a day off of work without her knowledge.

"What happened when you left your brother's house that night?"

"We drove home. The kids were both asleep so I first carried Jason inside and then Amy."

"Where was the Derringer pistol at that time?"

"It was in the glove box, but I removed it and took it into the house, placing it on a closet shelf where I routinely kept it. Anne had been screaming at me about having taken a day off of work, and when we arrived home and she found the note informing us that we had lost the bid on the house, her screaming resumed."

"Was you wife screaming words at you or just screaming? Krause asked.

"She was waving the letter in my face and calling me dumb and stupid. Then she started screaming orders at me.

"What kind of orders?"

"Oh, to clean up the kitchen, to check the children, and to get out," Tom said.

"And what did you do?"

"I started taking armloads of clothes out to my car, but then Anne started calming down and at one point said to me, 'You don't have to do everything I say.'"

"And then what happened?"

"I returned to the car and began taking the clothing back in, and it was then that I heard the shot. I ran back into the house. It was quiet and it smelled like gunpowder." Shaking his head, Tom said, "It was a weird situation. There was light from the TV and she was sitting in the chair."

"What did you do then?"

Here, Tom became teary as he said, "I went to my wife's side and shook her by the shoulder. I moved her head to the right, touched her chin and hair to look at her, and then panicked. I couldn't find the telephone, (although it was on a table alongside the chair containing his wife's body) and when I finally did find it, I dialed 911. Then I spotted Amy emerging from the bedroom so I ran to her and told her there had been an accident and asked her to take care of Jason."

"What happened when the police arrived?"

"They were unable to find the gun. I guess they thought I took it because I heard one of the officer say, 'He must have had something to do with it. Hold onto him.'"

"Did the police question you that night?" Krause asked.

"They argued more than questioned me. For over forty-five minutes they just kept asking me what happened and I became upset and enraged. I couldn't believe what they were doing, and they requested me to come to the police station, after which they would then take me to the hospital."

"What did you tell them happened?"

"I told the police I had been in the kitchen, checking the children, or outside, when I heard the shot. The police were insinuating that I was not telling the truth and I finally told them, 'I don't care what you put down,' I'm not going to argue with the police at three o'clock in the morning. Then I asked them, 'can I go now to the hospital now' and they said 'We will take you to the hospital after going to the police station.'"

"Tom, did you know that Anne's mother suspected you of killing her daughter?"

"No," Tom said, "I never thought that my mother-in-law

suspected me of killing her daughter. In fact, she wanted me to move in with her to be near Amy."

"Why do you think Mrs. Coar believes you killed her daughter now?"

"Because some family members saw me in a restaurant with Michelle "Bunny" Lyons and they thought I was with her, and I wasn't."

On cross, Fisher was both angry and aggressive.

"Your business, Electra-Sonic started going bad in November of 1979?"

"Around then, yes."

"What was the main problem with Electra-Sonic Mr. Hodgins?"

"It was a combination of things."

"A combination of things?" Fisher asked, raising his eyebrows. "Wasn't the main problem that you went out and bought a diamond ring, a Cadillac, and a Datsun, 280Z in October of 1979? Wasn't the main problem that you spent all the money?"

"That was not the problem!" Tom declared, flushing scarlet.

"You never delivered a furnace to Rita and Norman Wardell, did you?"

"I was going to use the one in their home for display."

"What was the problem with furnace delivery?"

"Unavailability."

"Did you ever return the Wardell's money?"

"I think, possibly."

"You never paid the rent on the Connell Building offices either, did you?"

"I stopped paying the rent when the business started going bad."

"You were subsequently evicted from those offices weren't you?"

"Yes, in April of 1980."

"How many people made complaints against you concerning Electra-Sonic?"

"At least seven people made complaints against me," Tom answered, quickly adding, "but some of them were paid back."

"Who paid those people back, Mr. Hodgins?"

"Cathy Green," Tom said reluctantly.

"Who paid for Anne's funeral?"

"Cathy Green."

"Who paid the funeral director?"

"Cathy Green."

"How did Mrs. Green pay for all of this?"

"With the proceeds from Anne's insurance policy."

"Oh, yes," Fisher said, nodding his head. "Anne had gotten in touch with Mr. Hicks to change the beneficiary on her life insurance, and the amounts on the large policies the two of you took out, didn't she?"

"Yes."

"And that made you angry, didn't it?

"It didn't make me angry, but I told her that partners should insure each other, not two other people."

"You called Cathy to your house after Anne died to discuss the insurance money didn't you?"

"No, the insurance meeting was held at my mother's home in order for Cathy to make a claim. I wanted to—and I would have—hired a pathologist to prove that it was an accident."

Of course he would have, I thought to myself. If he could have proved that, then Anne's death would have been worth fifty-thousand dollars to him.

"You moved Anne's body after she was shot, didn't you."

"I may have moved my wife's body a little when I touched her."

"You said you argued with the police for forty-five minutes, but it took you much longer than that to get to the hospital, why?"

"I called Anne's friend, Carol MacAndrew, to come take care of the children and had to wait for her to come from Factoryville."

"What occurred at the hospital?"

"I remember meeting with the donor people and signing the agreement, after which she was declared dead and taken to the operating room. There was lots of confusion. When I finally left, I went either to the Coars' or my mother's."

"You told this jury that you weren't romantically involved with Michelle Lyons when they saw you with her?

"Michelle stopped by the house to offer her sympathy. She

was a friend of Anne's."

"But you went on to marry Michelle Lyons, didn't you?"

"Yes," Tom said icily, "In June of 1981."

(In fact, Tom married Bunny only six weeks after Anne's death.)

"Sir, were you jealous of Anne?"

"No."

"Did you threaten Anne's life when you spoke to Janet Kalasinski?"

"No. I told Janet, 'If you don't stop it—the phone calls between Stanley and Anne—I will."

"You were looking for your wife's purse on the night she was shot, weren't you?"

"Yes."

"In fact, you were more concerned with finding that purse than with your wife's medical condition weren't you?"

"That's not true."

"Did you eventually find that purse?"

"Yes, on the porch."

"Anne had sold her car just that morning so there was a large amount of money in that purse wasn't there?"

"Yes," Tom hissed.

After Tom stepped off the stand, the defense rested. Fisher called two witnesses in rebuttal; Mrs. Alma Starr, the Hodgins landlady who testified that Tom and Anne had never negotiated to buy the house they were renting, and John Sanko of the criminal division of the clerk of Judicial Records who testified about complaints against Tom relating to his Electra-Sonic Company.

Closing arguments would commence the next day.

***

I felt confident that we had proven our case, and A.D.A. Bill Fisher appeared so too, as he stood to begin his closing argument on the morning of January 22, 1984.

"This case depends upon two things; circumstantial evidence and the credibility of Thomas Hodgins." Fisher used an analogy to explain circumstantial evidence to the jury. "Suppose you walked out of a movie theatre after a snowfall and saw a solitary set of footprints leading to a nearby store. If you followed the footprints and found one person in the store, you could determine beyond a reasonable doubt that this was the person whose footprints you followed. Well," Fisher continued, "There's snow and footprints in this case, too, and the footprints are of only one person; Thomas Hodgins."

Fisher reminded the jury of how Hodgins had portrayed himself during the trial as an old fashioned guy who believed in old-fashioned principles. "But this man," Fisher shouted, turning to point at the defendant, "left one woman with whom he was living, to marry the victim in 1980, while he was still married to yet another woman!"

The prosecutor went on to mention the many witnesses who had testified, and the numerous conflicting stories Tom had told about the shooting throughout the years. He ridiculed the defense's theory that "the right-handed victim shot herself with her left hand while sitting in a reclining chair."

Picking up the Derringer, he held the weapon before the jury. "Try and cock this gun with your non-dominant hand when you begin deliberations. You'll see how difficult it is. And don't forget, if Anne did shoot herself in the chair, the expert witnesses all testified that the gun would have recoiled from the chair and could not possibly have slipped down into the upholstery.

Implying that Tom was little more than a con-man, Fisher reminded the jury that he operated a "Deceptive, shady business that sold nine-hundred dollars' worth of nothing to one client, and five pieces of metal for eleven-hundred dollars to another. He deceived them," Fisher stressed, "And that shows him to be a deceiver!"

Lee Krause gave an impassioned plea for his client. "Tom Hodgins did not kill his wife," he said, likening the prosecution case to little more than "smoke, designed to cover up a lack of facts that allegedly show Hodgins shot his wife." Standing before the jury, Krause ended his argument by saying, "Tom Hodgins did not kill his wife. There's no evidence here, and by law, you must find him not guilty."

I was relieved when Krause finally sat down, feeling that he hadn't put so much as a dent in the prosecution's case, and then the judge began his charge to the jury. After Walsh spoke for approximately one hour, he announced to the jury that he would "sequester you if you do not come to a decision within a reasonable time today."

I could see the look of surprise on the jurors' faces and it bothered me. It was obvious that they had no desire to be sequestered. But it was when Judge Walsh told the jury that in order to "find the defendant guilty," they had to be convinced "beyond a reasonable doubt" that my heart sank. Had enough testimony been presented? It was a complicated case with a lot of technical testimony. Had the jurors understood it?

As the jury left to begin their deliberations, I couldn't shake the feeling of foreboding that overwhelmed me. After my family and I had spent a month in the Lackawanna County Courthouse, it was soon to be over, and I was terrified.

Early in the afternoon, the jurors sent out word requesting the testimony of the pathologists. That testimony had not yet been transcribed, and incredibly, there was no offer to read the testimony back to the jury. Within one hour of this, the jury announced that they had reached a verdict.

As the jurors filed in, Judge Walsh asked that the defendant stand, and then the verdict was read.

"We the jury, find the defendant, Thomas Hodgins *not guilty*."

Tom burst into tears at the words, as did his mother, who crossed herself with her rosary.

After a nineteen-day trial, Thomas Hodgins was found not guilty of first and third degree murder and voluntary and involuntary manslaughter.

I wept uncontrollably.

CHAPTER TEN

My mind reeling, I rushed out of the courtroom and down the steps. All I could think of was getting out of Scranton where murderers were allowed to get away with murder. The jury's words kept reverberating through my head; not guilty, not guilty, not guilty. I wanted to scream, rage, hit someone—anything—but instead, I ran away from that courtroom with all the dignity I could muster.

When the television reporters approached and shoved the microphone in my face, all I could say was, "I've got to believe there is justice somewhere. I've got to believe it, or I can't survive. There is a God above. 'Vengeance is mine,' saith the Lord." To another I said bitterly, "My family is so devastated. I just hope the Scranton police and the jury can sleep as well as we can. I just cannot believe it!"

Even after forty-one witnesses for the prosecution, the jury foreman, John Schofield stated, "It was the definition of circumstantial evidence and reasonable doubt that did it." Despite the fact that three forensic pathologists testified that they doubted Anne committed suicide, Schofield said, "They never really proved [Hodgins] did it."

The investigation had been bungled from the start, and the jury brought the issue home when they told the press that, "Dr. DeMaio's initial report stated, 'pending further police investigation,' but there was no investigation. What's wrong with our police department? There could possibly have been a different verdict if the police department had been more efficient. The police testimony was conflicting and it was evident that there was a lack of investigative procedures. This left doubt in our minds."

Tom's words for the press were, "I didn't do it, and thank God for everybody up there who believed me." Tom would not, however, be going home to celebrate. Instead, he was returned to the Lackawanna County Jail where he would await extradition to Ohio. There he faced a two-to-four year sentence for violating parole on a bad check charge. As he was led out of the courtroom, he mouthed the words, "I'll see you soon," to a woman who sat in the gallery. Perhaps his latest love?

Ann Nelson, too, faced the cameras that day, "I knew he didn't do it," she said of her son, "but I didn't think anyone else knew. Tom wasn't violent. I'm sorry for Mrs. Coar, but she had to know it wasn't true. I just wish she got Anne help when she needed it."

District Attorney Preate told the press that, "Hodgins had tried to plead to third degree murder the year before, but my office rejected it because the defendant wanted a seven year sentence that would run concurrent with the Ohio sentence."

Tom's lawyer strongly denied that his client wanted to plead, but I knew he had. A.D.A. Fisher had met with me in December 1983, in Stuart James' office to see if I'd agree to Tom's pleading guilty to third degree murder. Listening to Lee Krause now, I wondered if that had been just a dream.

***

The following Monday, when I returned to work after spending the whole month of January in the Lackawanna County Courtroom, I asked one of my employers, "Is that my whole year's vacation?"

"What you do on your vacation is your business," he replied.

His words upset and angered me, but I restrained myself. It would be a year and half before I got another vacation day. (Several years later, when this man had to have emergency bowel surgery and used his vacation time to do so, he commented to me, "What a way to spend your vacation." I could hardly refrain from saying, "What you do on your vacation is your business!")

The year 1984 had not had an auspicious beginning, nor did it improve. A week after Aileen returned home to Georgia—after being here for Tom's trial—she called to tell me that while she was gone her husband, wearing her Detective's Medical College of Georgia uniform and using her gun, had committed an armed robbery. Apprehended, he was soon jailed and now I had to face the fact that not only was there a murderer in my family, but a thief as well! Ashamed and embarrassed, I couldn't share this knowledge with anyone other than my children, but the arrest added stress and burdens I had not counted on. With her husband's imprisonment and the loss of his income I had to help Aileen and her two boys, Matt and Micah, financially. I advised Aileen to divorce him, for he was a definite deterrent to her career as a detective.

Each day, though a new beginning, became more painful to endure—but when I walked into the operating room, I dropped my personal feelings at the door, and smiled, even though my heart was breaking.

The first Monday in March, I was positioning an obese female patient on the table, and when I opened her mouth to intubate her, gastric contents came pouring out. I quickly suctioned and intubated her, but I was furious. Why had a patient come to the operating room with a full stomach for an elective dilatation and curettage (D&C)?

When I later found out that this woman had come to the operating room from the ICU where she had been taken previously after an episode of shock, I was really angry. When the patient died a week later, I became frightened as well. The autopsy revealed that she suffered from generalized familial polyposis, and that a polyp had penetrated from her stomach into her duodenum on Friday, thus necessitating her admission to the ICU. I had no clue of this—I had not examined her pre-operatively—it was the anesthesiologist who had cleared her for the operation, yet suddenly I was the bad guy. She had aspirated some acidic stomach contents on induction resulting in "Adult Respiratory Distress Syndrome." Facing a possible lawsuit and loss of my job I was truly angry and upset. Why was this elective surgery allowed to take place on this seriously ill woman? Was a D&C going to save her life?

Only one week later, I was assigned to give anesthesia to a seventy-five-year-old thin, debilitated female. The operation was being done to insert a femoral rod in her femur, and as I began preparations for the anesthesia, the patient turned to me and said, "I don't want this operation—I'm going to die."

I took extra precautions, determined not to allow such an outcome. We positioned her left side up, in anticipation of a left hip incision and rod insertion, and after a smooth, careful induction, the surgeon made the incision. As he reamed the femur, the electrocardiogram monitor straight-lined. Nothing is as dramatic as this sudden death. She had thrown an embolus—one of the hazards of bone fractures or surgery. We, of course, went through the motions of cardio-pulmonary resuscitation, doing everything expected in such cases, but it was useless. She died, just as she predicted she would. The helplessness one experiences is so overwhelming. The autopsy report showed generalized cancer, which again vindicated me, but her death affected me terribly, for Stan had had the same operation, and I was therefore "spooked" about doing the case. In addition to her pre-operative statement, she had been coerced into signing the operative permit by her son and the nurses. Why do we not respect the patient's wishes? Are we, who are in medicine, too unwilling to admit defeat over death?

No matter, my career was on the line, and as a result I suffered from extreme depression. This was the second incident in a week and I couldn't help but wonder if my judgment was clouded by my emotions. The stress was unbelievable. How would I provide for my children if forced to give up my life's work? My mother's constant reassurances that "It was her time" did not help.

My faith was sorely tried. Had there not been enough depressing and overwhelming tragedy done to me and my family? What more is going to happen that I cannot cope with, I wondered. Never have I prayed so earnestly, bombarding God with pleas. "Why are you allowing these things to happen to me? Please help me to understand what is happening to us." And, the most fervent; "Just help me get through the next hour, Lord" Eventually, with His help, the depression began to lift, but there were days and weeks and months of hell before it did.

CHAPTER ELEVEN

If, after the joyful birth of Anne on March 23, 1952, God had said to me, "To you, I give her, to love, teach, and enjoy, I would have replied, "I accept, and willingly agree, with no reservations, and am grateful for whatever time I will have with her." But even now, almost forty-years later, I still feel the pain writing about that time in my life, and I still ask God, "Why me?"

Of course, I know His answer; "Why not you?"

It was not until I lost Anne, that I suddenly realized all the tragedy my mother had endured in her life, and I marveled at the strength she must have had to accept the many heartbreaks life had dealt her. She lived through the Depression with four children and a sickly husband and worked hard her whole life without complaint. She survived the deaths of seven brothers and sisters, two husbands, her firstborn and only son, Paul, and her granddaughter, Anne. She prayed daily, and I know it was her faith that saw her through such bleak and tragic days.

My faith was strong too, and as I prayed during those awful, heart-wrenching days after Anne's death, Stan's death, and Tom's acquittal, I also spent many hours reflecting on my life and my children, pondering what I might have done differently in rearing them.

They were all so different, yet so close. The older ones had cared for, read to, and bonded with the younger ones. Each one of them, as they grew, exhibited the personality traits I see in them today, but unfortunately, with such a busy life, I did not appreciate their uniqueness back then.

Anne was never as sweet, loving and generous as Cathy. Instead, she was bold, brash, and daring. I remember one time, while living in Norfolk, we took the children to the beach and Anne wandered off. We were unable to find her, and just as we were about to call out the Coast Guard, sure she had drowned, a young man brought her to us from over a mile away! She was only about four-years-old at the time, and crying for her "Mommy."

Larry had been a good baby, seldom crying except when he was hungry. He was intensely studious, often sitting in the corner next to the chimney studying the Encyclopedia. He was an excellent student (top man in his class) and content to do his own thing. When Stan bought the motorboat after his mother's death in 1967, Larry became a real "Hot Dog" on it. He was able to take off from the dock on one ski, and never get more than his lower body wet!

Michael, on the other hand, was inquisitive, often dismantling anything mechanical, and now. to my delight, can repair or diagnose any problem mechanical or electronic.

Aileen, born four days after Christmas in 1957, was a loving, quiet, often aloof child.

Stan, Jr., "Chopper," was charming, smiling, and happy from the day of his birth. He loved trucks, cars and anything with wheels. His sisters adored him and pampered him while his brothers used him as the butt of their mischief. The boys were often heard to tell the story of how they put Chopper on his "tyke bike" and sent him down the hill adjacent to the house, across Main Street and down another hill when he was two-years-old!

Marilyn walked and talked early and was a pleasant, agreeable and extremely intelligent child. She was gifted, very mature for her years, and the most compassionate of my children. One day, when Stan was ill and I returned from the hospital, I said to Cathy, "Marilyn never asks how daddy is," and Cathy had said, "She doesn't have to, Mom, she can read it on your face."

Marilyn had been only twelve when Stan got sick, and having to adopt many of the roles normally done by adults had been forced to grow up far too quickly.

Nancy was a happy baby as well, and especially gifted in language and negotiating ability. I remember Stan referring to these two youngest girls as his "yidda yadies," because Marilyn could not say her L's—pronouncing them as D's—until she was three-years-old. That memory always brings a smile to my face.

I remember when I told my next door neighbor that I was pregnant with Nancy—at forty years of age—and she said to me, "She will be a comfort in your old age." How right she was! Although older when my two youngest children were born, Marilyn and Nancy did not allow me to get old. They kept me busy with band functions, ski trips, and vacations, and mingling with their young friends was an incentive to not allow grief to rule my solitary times, which were few and far between.

Stan and I were lucky that no major illnesses ever occurred among the children. Accidents and mishaps, yes, but nothing life threatening. Marilyn broke her collarbone one Easter Sunday when she slipped off a chair, and one time Michael, threatening Aileen over some TV program, caused her to fall and break her wrist when she tripped on a loose carpet. All of the children were daring. One day, as I drove toward our corner house I looked up and saw Anne sitting on the windowsill on the second floor—she had pushed the screen out! Another time, Larry had lifted the sewer grate to retrieve Anne's skate, and dropped it on his fingers, letting out blood curdling cries—there seemed never to be a dull moment in our lives.

Stan and I were exceedingly proud of all of them, and in a town which offered little for teens, they kept us busy. We never lacked for places to go or things to do. There were play rehearsals and music practice, orthodontic appointments, religious instructions, cheerleading, and basketball games.

The kids were all intelligent—both Marilyn and Larry were top students in their class. Just as Stan and I had always loved music, our children were musically gifted as well. Anne and Cathy learned to play the piano, Larry the guitar, Marilyn the clarinet and Nancy the trumpet. Often feisty, they all enjoyed singing on car trips and even today, singing around the campfire at the lake is one of our mainstays for entertainment.

There were constants evident in all our children—their

intelligence, their musical ability, and their athletic prowess. Anne was a dancer, Cathy, Aileen, and Nancy had been cheerleaders, and both Anne and Aileen excelled in gymnastics. Marilyn and Nancy have participated in many half times at football games in Shea Rich and other stadiums including Union-Endicott's Ty Cobb, where they performed in the two-hundred member marching band. They also marched in the Citrus Bowl parade in Florida, and performed for President Reagan when he came to Endicott. All, except Nancy, have performed in high school stage plays, and Larry and his friends practiced—and I'm sure disturbed—the neighbors with their rock band in our garage.

Michael displayed his first temper in the play "Flowers for Algernon" as the doctor, and Anne, as "Madame X" was outstanding. (I, as a juror could hardly be impartial in the portrayal of a sleazy woman on trial for the murder of a blackmailer who had discovered her secret background and threatened to expose her. At the trial, her defense lawyer was revealed to be her own son, but she refused to disclose this, and so was found guilty. Little did we know that Anne would be the victim of a murderer in only ten short years.)

At times, Stan could be a kid himself. I thought about that day in 1975, when Stan's sister, Nancy and I were basking on the deck at the Crystal Lake cottage. Stan came home from the night shift at IBM, but he wouldn't go in to sleep until he asked me to buy him a CB radio for Father's Day. Excitedly, he showed me a two-hundred and twenty-five dollar model in a catalogue.

"Where do you expect me to get two-hundred and twenty-five dollars? I asked.

Stan looked thoughtful, and then said, "Well, how much would you pay for one? A hundred dollars? Fifty? Twenty-five?"

Smiling, I said, "Oh, I'd probably pay twenty-five dollars."

With that, he got up from his chair and proceeded to take a CB radio out of the trunk of his car. He had seen it days before and bought it himself. "You can give me that twenty-five dollars now," he said with a grin.

Stan and I had so many memorable days at the lake in summer, and in winter, we had a ball traversing the countryside on our snowmobiles. One night, I fell off and Stan never missed me, returning only later to find me shivering in the snow. After that, I insisted we purchase a second snowmobile so that would never happen again!

Some of the best memories are just the small ones that bring a smile to my face. One evening when all of our children were sprawled over the furniture and floor in the family room, Stan came downstairs, looked around, and said, "Where is everyone?" (Meaning me).

Another time, during dinner, with six children seated on either side of the table, Michael asked to be excused and left the room.

Stan and I had become involved with the Forest City Ambulance Association and since he worked nights, he was the only male available to drive the ambulance during the day. I knew that a neighbor's boy had been involved in a snowmobile accident that morning and I asked Stan, "Did you take Andy Junior's son to the hospital today?"

"Yes," Stan answered.

"Whose snowmobile was he on?"

"I don't know," Stan shrugged. "I just know he hit a barricade and is in the ICU. I guess he's doing okay though."

That reminded me of something else I forgot to tell him. "Did you hear that Jack Pevec had a cardiac arrest in the ICU?"

Stan said he did, as he had transported him to the hospital while he was having symptoms. "Is he Mary Pevec's father-in-law?" He asked.

"Yes," I said, nodding my head.

With that, Mike came into the kitchen and asked, "Who had the cardiac arrest on the snowmobile?" That's now become a family question we jokingly ask when one misses details about a subject.

Another time, Larry called when we weren't home and Chopper answered. Informing us about the call, Chopper said Larry had called from 'Feableminster." This still brings a smile to my face: Larry then resided in Warminster.

It was easy to discern why many communications went unheeded or unanswered in our family. One of the favorite ploys of the teenagers was to listen to a question requiring a positive answer, and then quickly interject, "can I have the car tonight?"

When Stan or I answered, "yes" to the first question, the "car" questioner would promptly get up from the table and off in the car he'd go. With two babies who required feeding and caused distraction in those years, there was never any ongoing, meaningful conversation. Nancy, too, invariable spilled her milk at the dinner table, and oh, what I wouldn't have given for a Sippy cup in those days!

I remember one winter morning when I heard what I thought was a lawn mower. I wondered to myself, who in their right mind would be running a lawn mower in the dead of winter? Looking out the window, I saw it was Chopper. I should have known. He had rigged a board across the front of the lawn tractor and was plowing snow! Mischievous, daring and innovative, he would always help anyone in distress.

One day one of the nurses with whom I worked said to me, "Your son scared me half to death this morning."

"How?" I asked, frowning.

She proceeded to tell how, leaving for the hospital that morning in the cold darkness, she discovered her car had a flat tire. Chopper, then fourteen, was out on his paper route wearing my black snowmobile suit. Seeing the problem, he knocked on the car window and asked her, "Do you want me to fix it for you?" She nearly jumped out of the car with fright, but she was grateful.

I had to smile, too, when I thought about one Saturday evening when I had gone to the opera with some friends and returned home at midnight to discover I was locked out. Larry, home from college, finally awakened after twenty minutes of my pounding on the door, and sleepily remarked, "It's after 11:00 o'clock; do you know where your parents are?"

It wasn't only the children I reflected on, however. I thought about my entire life, including my career which had always meant so much to me. Before nursing school, my first and only experience with childbearing had been in 1946, when my sister Aileen was having young Russ. As her time to deliver approached, she stayed with Mom and Dad, while Russ Sr. worked in New Jersey. On January 28, Aileen went into labor, and I recall her sitting in the corner in the back bedroom of 161 South Main Street in Forest City, until Pop took her to the hospital. Then of course, while in nursing school my brother, Paul's wife, Eleanor, was in labor with Sharon, and Dr. MacAndrew asked me if I wanted to watch. Of course, I jumped at the chance, and seeing that child born had to be the most exciting event I had witnessed up until that time. I still find it amazing to think of my naivety, and the fact that I went on to have eight children of my own!

Nurses' training was a joy to me. I remembered one of the funniest things that happened was an incident involving one of my classmates, and her inability to get a female patient to retain the soap water enema she was trying to give. Coming out to complain to the supervisor about the patient's non-compliance, the supervisor took Rita out to the hall and said to her, "You're putting it in the wrong hole."

The Nightingale Sings

My roommates were Kay Bower from Hawley, and Marion Biglin, an Irish lass from Archbald. Marion had an Irish brogue that I could imitate perfectly. By the time we graduated and I relocated to Norfolk, I was so skilled in the Irish accent that one of Stan's buddies asked him, "When did your wife get off the boat?"

One night, still wearing my uniform, I sneaked out to meet Stan, who had driven thirteen hours from Norfolk to see me. At the time, we were not allowed to leave the dorm until morning and we were also not to wear our uniform off hospital grounds, so, going to a local hamburger joint, I refused to remove my coat. Finally, uncomfortable about possibly being seen, I told Stan to take me home to Forest City, for I had the next day off and would begin the day shift on Monday.

The following Monday, sailing down the hall with a patient's tray in my hands, I was halted by Sister Gilbert, the stern Director of Nurses, who startled me with, "Miss Walsh!"

I cringed, sure I'd been reported, and quaking, said, "Yes, Sister?"

"Where did you get those shoes?"

"I bought them in Baltimore, Sister."

"Well, go down to the nurses' home and take them off," she snarled.

I was so relieved not to be thrown out of training that I vowed never to do that—sneak out and not wear regulation uniform apparel—again.

My first day in the operating room was also very memorable,

for as the assistant at an amputation, I had to hold the leg while the surgeon sawed through the femur. For weeks afterward, I had nightmares and re-lived the experience in my sleep by sitting up in bed with arms outstretched. My roommates would wake me with the command, "Lie down, Anne, lie down."

Looking back at these times, I was amazed to realize how young, naïve, and innocent I was. A time when the most stressful thing in my life was risking being caught out of uniform. But it wasn't all fun and games.

I will never forget the hot, humid, summer day when I stepped out on the porch of the cottage at Crystal Lake and was startled by a thunderstorm moving across the water, accompanied by some very severe lightning. Only minutes later, the Clifford ambulance raced by the cottage, heading for the Golf course, one-half mile away. Thinking I might be of help, the older children and I jumped in the station wagon and followed. There we found a twenty-one-year-old doctor's son who had just stepped out of the Golf Shop and been struck by lightning. Placing him in the ambulance—at that time a hearse—his golfing partner, who happened to be a doctor, and myself performed CPR while we raced eighty miles-per-hour, over twisting roads to the hospital five miles away.

Meanwhile, Anne drove her sisters and the station wagon back to the cottage, and when Stan returned from Vandling Chopper reported to him gravely, "They took Mommy in the ambulance."

At the hospital, I intubated the young man while another

physician gave him an epinephrine injection directly into his heart. Trauma care was in its infancy at that time—nothing like the sophisticated administration seen today—and although we did our best for two hours, the doctor's son died of pulmonary edema, common among those struck by lightning. It was a freak accident; apparently stepping outside with the golf club over his shoulder, he was the tallest object in the area. His father, a cardiologist, was on his way to New York City but immediately returned to deal with the tragedy of his son's death, and for many years after, he conducted studies and research on death by lightning.

Another, once-in-a-lifetime career experience occurred late one night when I was called to the hospital to give anesthesia for an emergency caesarian section. I felt uneasy after the induction and initial incision, when I noticed the surgeon, attempting to grasp the baby, look sharply at the other assisting doctor. Their looks spoke volumes. Neither said anything, but as the surgeon pulled the babies out of the uterus we could all see that they were conjoined twins. (At that time, we referred to them as Siamese twins). They were connected face-to-face at the chest, and had only one heart to beat for them both. The circulating nurse took them to the bassinet and was told not to suction or attempt resuscitation, for they would not survive. They breathed on their own, but not for long, and my heart broke for the mother of these precious little souls. Today, of course, those babies would immediately be airlifted to the nearest pediatric surgery unit, where an attempt would be made to separate them, even if only one could have a chance to survive.

I was sad when St. Joseph's School of Nursing closed in 1978 after having graduated some 740 nurses. I had lost touch with my roommates from that time, Kay and Marion, but we met up again at our fifty year reunion to find that our lives had taken similar paths. We had all maintained careers while raising large families—five children for Kay, six for Marion, and eight of my own—and both Marion and I had buried our oldest child.

My reminiscing in the days, weeks and months after Tom's acquittal left me feeling sad and nostalgic, and longing for what had been. One of the most difficult things a person can do is accept the fact that things change, and somehow we must change with them. Nothing golden lasts.

CHAPTER TWELVE

The anger that raged in me after Tom's acquittal was like a cancer, eating away at me and driving me insane. I knew I would have to come to terms with what had happened—even forgive Tom—if I were to survive. I worked at it daily, and as the years passed, things finally began to take on a more normal routine.

On October, 10, 1987, my son, Mike and his fiancé, Diane Reed were married in a lovely ceremony at the Gazebo in Kennedy Park, followed by a reception at the Belmont Fire Hall. The following St. Patrick's Day their daughter, Jessica was born prematurely at Wayne Memorial Hospital. I quickly sewed a number of preemie nightgowns and kimonos for her, for they were not prepared for an early arrival.

Also in 1987, Marilyn graduated from Union-Endicott high School and prepared to go off to college at Penn State. Physically, I could not bear to leave her there, so Chopper transported her and her belongings to the dorm. I wept for two days.

Marilyn's room did not remain vacant for long, however. Anne's daughter, Amy soon occupied it. Anne and I had been pregnant at the same time, and although Amy and my daughter, Nancy were only a month apart in age, Nancy was Amy's aunt. The girls really enjoyed the looks of confusion from the other kids at Union-Endicott high School when Nancy would introduce Amy as her niece.

In June 1989, Nancy and Amy graduated, and we prepared for

the traditional graduation party at the cottage on Lewis Lake. Arriving there the night before we found the creek over which we had to drive impassable. It had disappeared due to the breakage of a dam upstream! This necessitated moving all the food back to New York, but the party went off well, and the girls made preparation to depart for college.

With each child's leaving, either to marriage, college or into the service, I experienced tremendous separation anxiety, but nothing as prevalent as when Amy and Nancy left for college. I was sixty-four-years-old, and, for the first time in *fifty-nine years*, truly alone.

Amy entered the State University at Cortland, but Nancy applied to Penn State and attended her first year at the Altoona campus. Marilyn consistently made the Dean's List and had become engaged to a fine young man named John Dolly.

One day, Marilyn accompanied Nancy and me to Altoona where Nancy was scheduled for pre-admission testing. Marilyn and I decided to shop for her wedding gown while Nancy took her tests. Altoona is a town of one way-streets with similar names such as First Street, First Avenue and First Lane. Soon, the two of us became so disoriented I was almost in tears. Finally, we decided to park and take our chances on foot. The moment Marilyn stepped out of the car, a bird defecated on her bright blue blouse! It took us forever to find the Bridal Shop, but after purchasing a dress, we came out of the store only to find that our car had disappeared. I thought someone had stolen it, but we were just so disoriented that we discovered we were looking on the wrong street. Finally, after a stressful and nerve-wracking day we retrieved Nancy and snaked our way out of Altoona. Driving down a one-way street we saw a church sign which read, "Do you know where you're going?" We all erupted into laughter as I shouted, "No, I don't know where I'm going!" It was exactly what was needed to at last break the tension.

By her second year of college, Nancy was admitted to the main campus at Penn State, where Marilyn had gone, and some of my happiest times occurred there; going to the ballet, eating ice cream at the Creamery, sleeping in the dorm, breakfasts at Ye Olde College Diner and of course, shopping with the girls.

Marilyn and John Dolly had married in September of 1990 and on January 12, 1992 Marilyn graduated from Penn state on the Dean's List. I was so proud of her, for she already had one child, Elijah and was graduating just one month shy of giving birth to her second baby, Jackson. It had not been easy, either emotionally or financially, but with the Dolly's help and support, and mine, Marilyn and John were now ready to go out and face the world. I felt a sense of satisfaction in having gotten another child out of college, and as they marched to the front of the gym, I have to admit I saw no one else but my daughter. Tears of happiness and pride obscured my vision, and I thought about how proud and happy Stan would have been of all our children.

After Stan died, I had taken Marilyn and Nancy out of the Forest City School system, where they had attended for eight years and forged strong friendships, and thrown them into a totally foreign environment in Union-Endicott Schools where designer jeans identified one. I never knew until later how unhappy Marilyn had been by my decision to do this.

How I regret not being a more observant parent, but if one learns from experience, good or bad it's to one's advantage. Now, as a mother, Marilyn is extremely sensitive to her children's reactions with their school situations. Any problems are immediately nipped in the bud simply by her having good communication with their teachers. I prayed that John and Marilyn would settle here in Endicott, but John's parents offered them a home and job in Gettysburg, and so they relocated there after Jackson's birth.

Nancy and Amy were both still in college, so with everyone away on weekends I was footloose and fancy free. I frequently traveled to Forest City to visit my Mom and take her out to dinner. Andy Crowley, my old square dancing partner who I continued to see, often accompanied me on Sundays, but he owned a hardware store and that was the only day it was closed. The freedom of not having customers gave him time to do whatever needed to be done at the store and so, more often than not, I traveled alone. My life had never been dull, and it still wasn't. Andy and I subscribed to season's tickets for the Tri-Cities Opera and the Binghamton Symphony, and I was still singing with the B.C. Pops. With rehearsals every Sunday I had a busy social life plus, I was still working.

Throughout the years, I had watched the medical profession advance, but the one drawback, in my opinion, has been that doctors have become unwilling to let nature take its course. This is especially true where the terminally ill or the elderly are concerned, and where too many attempts at extraordinary means are used to keep one alive beyond one's time. In fact, this has created much distress with my feelings, leading to one of the most embarrassing moments in my life.

One Friday morning I arrived in the dressing room and found no pants in my size except one which was missing one of its drawstrings. No matter, I thought, as I fastened the waist with a large needle, and proceeded with my day's work. At 2:30, one of the doctors called to me and said, "Annie, go set up in room nine. We have a patient coming in for a feeding tube insertion." Inquiring about her condition, he related that she was an "ASA 3"—a fairly sick patient, who had a brain tumor, was barely conscious, and had been brought from the nursing home for this procedure. My thinking was "let nature take its course," but I did my job and prepared to give her IV sedation and monitor vital signs. I knew this might give her, at best, a few more days—but of what use? In a fetal position, barely conscious, she was not going to enjoy these tube feedings which might even prolong her pain, and her family's agony of watching her die. I knew it was certainly not going to improve her quality of life.

As the orderlies transported her into the room, I was even

more disgruntled about doing this case. The patient was curled in a fetal position, moaning, and non-responsive. As I placed the EKG leads on her chest, and the blood pressure cuff on her left arm, I saw that she had a naso-gastric tube inserted in her nose for present feeding, and an intravenous infusion in her right hand. I needed to see that this site was adequate enough to withstand large doses of medicines through the needle in anticipation of cardio-pulmonary resuscitation. She also had bandage restraints on her wrists to prevent her pulling out the needle or tube, necessitating that I cut through these to check the needle site, and as I was doing so, I cut through the intravenous tubing, and the fluid started spewing all around us. Angry with myself for such stupidity, I proceeded to restart the IV, and was then ready to begin the administration of the medications. I rechecked her blood pressure, heart rate, and IV flow but then noticed that her naso-gastric tube had fallen out of her nose onto the floor. Reaching over her extended left arm to retrieve it, the pin at my waist popped open and my pants fell to my ankles just as the surgeons came through the door with hands scrubbed, ready to proceed with the operation.

As I reached to the floor, to pick up the pants, I reddened, and wished the floor could open up and swallow me, but the doctor didn't seem to mind. "Okay, let's go," he called.

On March 8, I received another dreadful phone call informing me that my son, Michael had been in a drunk-driving accident totaling his car and sustaining head and neck injuries. Rushing to the hospital in Carbondale, I found him belligerent, unhappy, and in terrible pain. It was then that I became aware that another of my family members was a victim of alcoholism. Organizations such as MADD (Mothers against drunk driving) had formed in the 1980's but had not achieved the prominence they have today in influencing legislation, so Mike didn't bear the consequences of his actions. It's possible that if he had, the ensuing years might have been better for him. Instead, his drinking escalated after this accident, just as Stan's had when he approached his forties and as a result, dire consequences ensued. These included divorce and estrangement from his family, job losses, more DUI's—in both Pennsylvania and New York—and imprisonment for non-support of his daughter. Mike's drinking culminated in the total breakdown of his life, during which the family and I stood by helplessly, trying to "solve" the problem with financial and emotional support, but to no avail.

Later in that same month, Nancy was also in an accident. While driving a friend's truck she had struck a tree, but was not hurt. Again I shuddered to hear the phone ring.

In May, while starting an intravenous on a patient who was scheduled for eye surgery, I suddenly felt weak and collapsed on the floor. Transported to the emergency room, doctors discovered my blood sugar was reading 350, and I was diagnosed with diabetes mellitus. This began a real period of depression over my own mortality, and concern with what effect it would have on my life. Though I had suspected I had the disease, for I had experienced symptoms—extreme thirst, frequent urination, irritability and shakiness, in addition to extreme hunger, even though losing weight—I wasn't worried, nor had I made an appointment to see a doctor.

The previous Tuesday, however, I'd been traveling to Cortland to take Amy out to dinner, and had experienced profound weariness, almost falling asleep at 4:00 p.m. I had a bag of candy in the car and after eating some, experienced immediate relief of my tiredness. Therefore, I suspected there was a problem with my metabolism.

I began to watch my diet and exercise, and eventually obtained control of my blood sugar, but it has resulted in many problems in my schedule. Eating, checking blood sugar daily, and walking have become a focus of regulation. Several times I felt I might lapse into a coma—which is scary—and often, if I haven't eaten, or eaten the wrong thing, I feel out of control. When one is confronted with a serious disease such as this, one must learn how to live and deal with it daily. Like most diseases, though, one cannot know what damage is being done to eyes, heart, or kidneys.

After Anne's death, and with this diagnosis, I appreciate every day for what it brings, and am thankful for another sunrise in my life and the ability to deal with the day's events—as my mother did—with equanimity.

***

Andy and I had begun to travel in 1991. In June, we rented a condo in the Laurentian Mountains in Canada and ventured into Montreal to see Nana Moskourri in concert. Traveling seventy-five miles-per-hour one afternoon on the interstate, Andy felt something wrong, and so we stopped at a Michelin tire shop, where a huge slash was discovered in the right front tire. After replacing the tire, we continued back to the resort where we both breathed a sigh of relief. Another angel had been watching over us; if the tire had blown, we probably would have been killed.

In September, we flew to Ireland, departing from New York at 9:00 p.m. and arriving at Shannon Airport at 3:00 a.m. After disembarking, I had the feeling I had "come home." Ireland was a beautiful, peaceful country. The people, with their unfailing enthusiasm, Irish brogues, genuine hospitality, and musicianship, enchanted us, making it one of the most memorable events of my lifetime. During our first night there, sitting in the moonlight on the shores of Lake Killarney, I said to Andy, "I thought we might get married in Ireland."

"Me, too," Andy replied, but nothing more was said and the subject was dropped. It would take five more years before we exchanged vows!

We visited every castle, cathedral and pub, and stayed at a different hotel every night. We marveled at St. Katharine's Cathedral, shopped at the Waterford China Factory, toured the National Library in Dublin, and Andy even kissed the Blarney Stone. I still recall our trip to Ireland as one of the happiest times in my life. It saddened me to leave, for I had truly fallen in love with my grandparents' native land and hope to return again one day.

On Friday, October 3, we took a trip to Forest City where my sister, Florence informed us that Mom had fallen off a curb in Carbondale and was in the hospital with a head injury. We rushed down to see her, and it was the last time she knew me for months. She had sustained a hematoma and with the hemorrhage inside her skull putting pressure on her brain, she became another person. She had short term memory loss and suffered many complications common to head injuries, including petit mal seizures.

I had no idea of the enormity of her trauma. I went down and stayed with her in the I.C.U. for the next two days, sitting with her, bathing her and taking care of her. On Saturday, she shocked me when she lashed out at me. Pointing her finger in my face, she began screaming, "You! You put that rug back"

"What rug?" I asked.

"My rug," she screamed. "I know you're cleaning out my apartment! Put that rug back!" As I sat there in horror, I realized that this injury had created a mother I never knew, and things didn't get better over the ensuring days.

The building hematoma had begun draining under the skin to her throat. During that week the surgeon drained it twice, externally, but she continued to bleed. With the increasing pressure on her brain, it became more difficult to ambulate her. On Thursday, I got her out of bed to walk the hall, and while trying to get her off the commode, almost dislocated my shoulder. It took myself, and two other nurses to get her back into bed.

It was an incredibly stressful time, not only because of mom's condition, but because of problems with my sisters as well. I knew the doctors would discharge my mother soon, and both Florence and Aileen had decided that I should give up my employment and take her home with me. I realized that Mom would require twenty-four hour-a-day nursing care, which would require lifting, changing, and feeding, but when I confronted Aileen with the prospect of a nursing home, she was unable to grasp the enormity of this kind of care. She felt I could, and should, do it. I was angry, and adding more fuel to the fire was the fact that she took off to spend a week in Las Vegas.

By the end of the week, Mom's condition had deteriorated badly. She was now being medicated for the petit mal seizures, but on the following Wednesday, the doctors were talking about discharging her.

My sister Aileen was leaving for Florida on November 1, which would leave Mom's care in the hands of me and Florence. Florence was unable to make room for her, and besides, she drove a school bus, so the logical person to take her was me. Aileen offered to take her to Florida for three weeks, and then send her back to me to take care of for the rest of her life.

The next day, Mom had a seizure and became violent and angry. Later, however, she seemed more like her old self. It was scary—what was happening to my mother? The next day, she was transferred to Allied Rehabilitation Center but her left leg was not moving well—she'd had some neurological damage. I was still working, and only able to get there in the evenings, so never had a chance to communicate with Mom's doctors. If my sisters communicated with them, they didn't inform me.

The next Saturday, I spent the entire day with Mom. She was hostile and angry when I got there, but later became calmer. Her appetite was very poor, though, and this concerned me, for often when humans are about to die, they cease eating. The next week, we had a conference with the staff, which held no high expectations since Mom had had another seizure and was very childlike. I had to wonder if it was the drugs or the injury causing this. They were apparently giving her so much Dilantin and Phenobarbital that it was affecting her mental state, and she continued to eat poorly. Within the week, she became very depressed and had a Doppler test for phlebitis. What next, I wondered?

On the following Friday, Aileen, Florence and I had a conference with the doctors, physical therapists, dietician, and Social Services Department. They informed us that Mom would need twenty-four hour care—probably in a nursing home. The following Tuesday, she was moved back to St. Joseph's Hospital because she'd developed clots in both her legs. She cried and moaned with pain and I wept as I drove home, feeling both helpless and hopeless. I took the next two days off and stayed with her, but found it emotionally draining. How does one deal with a parent becoming a child? I stayed at her apartment that weekend, not wanting to drive back to Endicott, and spent the day with her, bathing and changing her. At least it made me feel as if I were doing *something*. On Sunday, she threw a clot to the lungs and became dysenteric, cyanotic and very agitated. What next?

The next day she was again confused and agitated. She'd had another CT scan, which showed nothing. Now the doctors prescribed Ativan for the agitation, but it rendered her almost unconscious. I didn't know this, and upon seeing her, thought, "Has she had a stroke?" I would have objected had I asked the nurses what they had begun to administer. Mom hated drugs and never took them. Months later, when I realized that she should have healed but was still confused and talking strangely, I told them to take her off all the drugs and she became her old self.

On November 5, Mom finally recognized me, and it was so heartening. She was actually lucid and pleasant, but she'd been in the hospital for four weeks, and had begun to develop bedsores. Things had not improved in my relations with my sisters either. None of us ever sat down with each other, or Mom, relevant to making a decision. Unhappy emotions could so easily be avoided if family members would just sit down with each other and discuss plans to take care of an ailing parent, rather than assume that one or the other is the logical one to undertake the full-time care of such. My anger escalated when Aileen came home from a five-month stay in Florida, and announced, "We're closing Mom's apartment this weekend." There had been no discussion about this. No one asked if I could be available, and no one called to say, "Hey, we're going down to go through Mom's things. Do you want anything?"

At the same time, I was having confrontations with one of the other nurse anesthetists at my job. She was taking advantage of lunch hours—sleeping for an hour after eating a quick lunch, thus forcing me to do lunch relief. She was also lying to the anesthesiologists, asking for prime time vacations and, in general slouching on her duties, which forced me to assume some of hers.

What I would have given for some means to communicate with Mom, and for some company on the long, lonely dark trips through the winters of 1992-93. Many nights I came home in tears, and although Andy waited until 11:00 p.m. for me, he was always asleep, or preparing to go to his apartment. He never asked how Mom was, nor was I able to communicate my concern to him. All I could do was tumble into bed.

I had also begun to develop cataracts but I didn't know it. I surely knew, however, that with my night vision and uncontrolled blood sugar, I was a definite hazard to myself and others on the highway. Everything was hazy, blurry, and the green exit signs were no longer green.

We had to make a decision about Mom, and again, my faith was sorely tried. What was my duty? What was my obligation? Should I retire, and take care of her full-time? Could I physically take care of her? In my heart I knew the answer was, "No." Not without help.

I was a nurse, but there was no way I could physically lift her, walk her, and take care of her alone. I now know that not only was she brain damaged, but the effort to get out of chairs, off the commode, or even stand up, was too difficult without the proper aid. It was a difficult decision to make—to put one's loved one into a nursing home amounts to abandonment in most everyone's mind, but one also has to be realistic.

Aileen's plans were to go to Florida with her husband for the next four months, taking Mom for three weeks, and Florence's was to continue to visit Mom, but the whole burden of her care would have been on me. I knew that moving her into my home, where she had no friends or family other than myself, would be very depressing for her. Mom was a "people" person. Ultimately, I know it was the right decision. Mom had lived in Forest City for ninety years. She knew everyone there.

On December 7, she was transferred to the Forest City Nursing Home, and the first time I went down to visit she seemed better, although her arms and legs were again darkened in color.

The first ray of hope for her recovery came on December 16, when the "Polka Jets" entertained at the nursing home Christmas party and Mom laughed and sang along. That night, I drove home singing too.

Always alone on these excursions to the Nursing Home, I often cried to see my mother in this situation. Mom was always a beautiful person, not only in appearance with her jet black, naturally wavy hair and green eyes in her youth, but also in her demeanor. She was always beautifully dressed, with her jewelry in place. She was personable, unassuming, and well-liked and, after the death of her husbands, she enjoyed traveling with friends and family, shopping, and attending daily Mass. After my father's death, she ran his fuel oil business and worked in the Endicott Johnson shoe factory. Though she never owned her own home, she was a spotless housekeeper and good cook, having the whole family for Christmas dinner, until she was in her eighties. Her pie baking was legendary, for in the 1940's, when she worked as a waitress and cook at her sister-in-law, Agnes' restaurant, she baked as many as seventy-five pies a week, scrubbed the floors, cooked, and waited on customers for one dollar a day.

She had always enjoyed good health until now. She'd had a pacemaker inserted at age sixty-five when she finally admitted her age to me for the first time. Concerned about how she was going to pay for the operation, I asked her and she airily replied, "Oh, I'm on Medicare now."

She'd walked daily, to the store and Mass, and volunteering was her way of life. Until she was eighty-five, she planned the funeral breakfasts and St. Patrick's Day dinners in the church basement. She had begun volunteering early. At age sixteen, during the world-wide flu epidemic, she nursed the sick and dying in the makeshift hospital in the old Forest City High School. She related how "the coffins were stacked in the corner awaiting burial," and recalled that one-hundred and fifty people died in Forest City at that time. She was so independent! Even after a fractured hip, at age eighty-nine, she was able to continue living alone. She was the treasurer of the Senior citizens' organization and many fund-raisers locally, and was very well-liked.

Mom was a realist too. I remember one day I called and told her how we had saved a heart attack victim at work with our magnificent resuscitation efforts, and that he was now recovering in ICU. As excited as I was, Mom immediately burst my balloon with, "It wasn't his time to go."

Mom helped to keep me in line with my career and remind me that I was only God's instrument in patient's recoveries. I always began every day with a prayer for God to guide my hands to administer to the patient safely.

Now here was this ever independent woman, unable to leave the nursing home. She still tried to, though. Occasionally she would attempt to climb over the bedrails and I would find her with large bruises on her arms. At one point, I also discovered that the staff was restraining her with a straitjacket.

In April, some friends who had not seen Mom prior came for a visit and immediately said to me, "She's being overmedicated." I had no clue it was the drugs making her behave so peculiarly; I thought it was the result of the head injury. I had no concept that she was being overmedicated, and I went to the nurses and ordered the doctor to remove all medications. Slowly, Mom began to revert to her old self again. She still had lapses of memory, and sometimes the inability to express her thoughts, but she was better.

That Christmas was marred by Mom's being in the nursing home. I could not take her out, as she was in a wheelchair and not lucid at times. Carrying our gifts, we visited her in the home and then the family traveled to Aunt Marilyn's house, as we had for the past thirty-five years. It seemed Christmas was the only time for my large family to reunite. One of the highlights of the evening was gathering around the piano after dinner and singing Christmas carols, wishing for it to never end. They were such fun and memorable times with the children, and now the grandchildren, gathering. I remember driving home with Christmas music playing, and often snow falling and experiencing such gratitude that all was well with our family.

Mom was doing well enough that I took her on Sunday outings. We'd go to Mass, do some shopping and then dine out, which she enjoyed. I also took her to the cottage for the day on weekends, and we'd stop by at Florence's for a visit on the way back.

Mom would spent almost two years in the nursing home, but she had improved, even becoming the President of the Residents Association. However, she was never able to live alone again. I remember when she discovered that we'd dismantled her apartment. It was a devastating experience for her, but after the initial shock, she rallied. We even discussed her going into the skilled nursing facility which was then being constructed adjacent to the nursing home.

On September 19, 1994, however, the day of the open house for this new facility, Mom suffered a stroke and died four days later. The night before she passed away, I had a terrible choice to make. My son Mike had been arrested for non-child support and I had to choose whether to go visit him in jail or stay with my dying mother. Visiting hours at the jail were only on Tuesday and Thursday evening from 7:00 to 7:30 so I decided to visit my son. My reward for this gesture was his terrible anger. Hoping Mom would survive until morning, I drove home in tears, and awoke the next morning to a shrilling phone and the voice of my sister saying, "Mom just passed away." I regret to this day I did not stay with her, for she died alone. We had maintained almost twenty-four hour vigils during her final days and my sister-in-law was on her way to sit with Mom, but she didn't arrive in time and Mom died alone.

This was almost the most stressful condition I had ever endured. To see one's parent regress to childhood, and yet respect the parenthood, has to be one of the most difficult situations with which one can cope. And, having prayed and sat with so many dying patients, the fact that my mother died alone is, and has become, almost unbearable for me. It has helped to create a rift in my relationship with my son, which is now almost non-existent. "How sharper than a serpent's tooth is an ungrateful child."

With Mom's death, I became an elder in the family. The loss

of one's mother creates a void totally irreplaceable. No matter how loving or tenuous the relationship, there is no longer anyone who will be your mentor, friend, confidante, critic, or champion. No matter what the child does, the child will always remain in the mother's heart and thoughts—never ceasing to be her child. I often found myself teary-eyed remembering Mom, and now time often hangs heavy on Sunday, as I had no reason to go home again to Pennsylvania.

My relationship with my mother had always been tenuous; she never seemed to approve of me, my choice of husband, or my children, and she was critical of everything I did. This had always bothered me, but one day, dealing with these emotions at the cemetery—where God and I conducted our most meaningful conversations—I encountered a former teacher and friend who altered my perception of Mom's and my relationship. She assured me that Mom had often told others about my caring for her—taking her to the hospital for battery changes in her Pacemaker, doctor's visits, and of her becoming sick one night and me staying with her the whole time.

I did try to be good to my mother. When her second husband died of congestive heart failure, I left my family on Mother's Day to be with her, and helped her through that trying time. Another time, when Mom had been in bed with dizziness for a week, my brother, Paul asked me "What are you going to do about your Mother?" I got on the phone, and had her transferred to Packer

Hospital in Sayre, Pennsylvania, where she was diagnosed with Meniere's disease.

My brother and sisters seemed to think that even though I had a fulltime job and eight children, I should also assume care of my mother, and I often did, frequently leaving my children alone when Stan worked third shift.

Mom was never a complimentary or demonstrative person, but why couldn't she have told me just one time that she loved or admired me? The last time I had her for dinner at the cottage, two weeks before she died, she complimented me by saying "You know, you're a good cook," and I was thrilled.

In reflecting now, I realize that Mom felt very intensely about me and prayed often for me. A mother's prayers are always answered, and although I was not given an easy life, I was given tremendous strength to cope with whatever I was dealt. I pray only to accept whatever occurs, placing all in God's hands, knowing that He knows all, sees all and will allow what is best for me.

The hard work of rearing eight children, working full-time, often being on-call at the hospital, and dealing with an alcoholic husband must have concerned her, for I too, as a parent, feel all the happiness and pain of my children's lives. I have also come to realize that, as a parent, one can only guide the child to do his best and hope for happiness in their lives, but they must make their own choices whether we agree with them or not.

I know Mom loved me in her own way, and before she died, while she was still aware, I was able to tell her that I loved her too.

CHAPTER THIRTEEN

On May 20, 1994, shortly before Mom's death, my daughter, Nancy and her love, Nicholas English, were married in a beautiful ceremony at St James Church in Johnson City. The event was the culmination of my dreams, for what mother does not yearn to see her daughter, especially her baby, walk down the aisle adorned in bridal white, as she never will be again? The reception at the Kalurah Temple was attended by over 150 happy people, and was to be the last time my whole family would be together. After Larry moved to Key West, it seemed impossible to gather everyone together again.

Each spring, I would contemplate selling my cottage on the lake. My health was deteriorating and the responsibility of two homes was overwhelming, but no one wanted to see it go. The children would come to help me open and close it and it has since become the focus of family reunions every summer.

Andy, too, took a great deal of interest in my summer home and took it upon himself to clear away all the brush and overgrown trees, and then plant flowers and vegetables which I still can each summer.

Andy's tree cutting has become a subject of many discussions. He loves landscaping and gardening and accomplishes these with thoroughness, spending hours and days digging out tree stumps. No amount of hard work intimidates him, but his tree-cutting has become a legend. At one point when I mentioned we needed to trim a tree or two to obtain some sun on the vegetable garden, he chopped down six! He has beautified the grounds with his hard work, and grown many organic veggies for our table. I laughed when he told me the story of being a youngster and spending the summer at the Crowley cottage at Ouquaga Lake. Wood was needed for the fireplace, and Andy decided to get some, felling a tree across the highway! When he cut trees at my cottage, he would enlist my help in holding the ladder, but one day, misdirecting a branch, he dropped it on my head and I informed him that I no longer would be anywhere nearby when he dropped a tree!

Andy still owned his successful business in New York, and we attended annual hardware shows in the Poconos, eventually buying a time-share condo and spending time there with Marilyn, Nancy, and their families, as well as our friends, Don and Carol Cox.

In 1994, we planned another trip to the West, and flew to Seattle where we stayed overnight with Andy's brother, Bob, his wife, Janice, and their daughter, Keira. We had a wonderful time, attending a wooden boat show and renting a Subaru to motor through the Cascade Mountains. Traveling to the Rocky Mountains, we arrived at Lake MacDonald Lodge in a rainstorm and awoke to find six inches of snow on the ground, sparkling like diamonds in the brilliant sunshine. The Rocky Mountains were incredible, and upon seeing them, I thought to myself, "How can anyone say there is no God?" Their beauty also inspired me to use the adjective 'awesome' for the first time in my life!

On that trip we also visited Yellowstone National Park, where we arrived in time to see the geyser erupt in all its beauty and majesty, and where Andy took photo after photo of buffalo, elk and moose. Seeing bubbling mud and hot springs boiling over, we were fascinated by nature's activities.

We drove back to our condo in Sun Valley, and since horseback riding was offered—and I thought I was seventeen—I asked Andy if we could take a ride up into the Sawtooth Mountains. As I sat upon an old white nag, it occurred to me that this did not resemble the days when I galloped on "Pete" over the hills of Pennsylvania! With every stumbling movement of that horse I pictured myself pitching over her head and down the mountain! Relieved to arrive back at the stall in one piece, I was rather bow-legged and suffered from saddle sores for a day. Andy, however, had no complaints. Finally at age sixty-five, I was cured of another dream; to become a "wild westerner!"

After driving to Boise, Idaho, where we attended a real Western rodeo, we flew to Washington, D.C. where our flight was grounded for four hours. Larry and Maureen were living in Crystal City so we called them and they surprised us with a visit.

My appetite for travel had been whetted by this trip, and so, the following spring we traveled to the Smoky and Blue Ridge Mountains, and to Asheville, North Carolina where we toured the area and sights. We than traveled to Augusta, where we enjoyed a few days with Aileen and her family, going to her in-laws for dinner, which included Ed Jackson's "famous turnip greens and pork."

Springtime is to savor in the South. As we drove East to visit with Andy's sister Joanne, and her husband, John Bonestell in Charlotte, and then on to see Bernetta and Bill Doolittle in Wilmington, the sight of the blooming dogwoods among the hemlocks and pines brought back many memories of my favorite time in Norfolk. After a memorable visit with them, during which the folding bed folded up with me in it, causing us to double over in laughter, we then visited Norfolk, and several old friends there, including the Wendells and the Wagners. We toured the Azalea Gardens, (now Norfolk Botanical Gardens), and I recalled the many times Elaine Buley, Jan, Lola, and I spent picnicking in these gardens, fifty years ago. In fact, at one of our picnics, on March 29, 1954, Elaine went into labor with Jan, but declined to tell us because she didn't want to miss the fun. She figured there were two nurses among us who could deliver her, should she require it!

This was a trip "down memory lane" for me. The gardens were no longer the simple paths through wooded pine-treed acres of tulips, daffodils and flowering shrubs in which we had picnicked with the children. Today, the manicured, winding paths are professionally tended and groomed, including the mirror pool, with a walk-around and flowers surrounding it where, in the 1950's, I was the Bromley Garden club President.

In December of 1995, I experienced profound pain in my right knee and after taking an X-ray, the doctor pronounced, "You need to have a total knee replacement." Giving me an injection of procaine and cortisone, I went home to ponder this life changing development. I was not prepared for total or partial disability, nor giving up my profession. Although I was sixty-five, retirement plans only hovered on the horizon—this was reality!

Two days later, while walking in the hall at Wilson, the knee locked and then swelled so bad that there was no walking on it. One of the orthopedic surgeons examined me and said "Yes, you need a total knee replacement."

With Andy pushing me in a wheelchair out of the operating room, experiencing pain I'd never imagined, I mumbled a silent prayer, "Please don't let my career end this way." But it did. On December 12—the fourteenth anniversary of Stan's death—I underwent surgery and a total knee replacement and was never able to resume administering anesthesia again.

The recovery period was most depressing; for over the next three weekends we suffered three blizzards, rendering us totally "snowbound." The fourth weekend, a flood occurred, when the sun finally came out and melted all the snow. The weather prevented my children from visiting me during the recovery period, making me extremely depressed. My son, Michael, however, was then residing with me, so I was never alone. Snowed in, he prepared meals, did the laundry and cleaning, and was available should I need someone. He was a godsend, but still, I lapsed into a terrible depression. The sudden life change, the constant, unrelenting pain, the total confinement to the house, no visitors and walking on crutches was probably one of the worst periods of my life. Never having had time to myself, I felt guilty about "doing nothing" all day. Andy, too, was available to help, but felt helpless, when the pain became too intractable.

Initially, retirement was a really enjoyable, long-awaited event. I was able to spend a whole summer at the cottage on the lake, but I was lonely too. I realized that without direction and motivation to get out of bed and dress, one can fall into rather slovenly habits.

In November 1996, I decided to add on a sewing room and new deck to my home, but I ended up falling and injuring my left knee. Doctors told me that knee, too, had deteriorated and so, on May 20, 1997 I underwent my second painful surgery to replace that knee as well. Constant pain hounded me for over five weeks and I was convinced I would never be pain-free again. But I considered myself lucky just to be able to walk.

During this time, my daughter, Marilyn nursed me, and a better nurse one could never find. Marilyn was kind, caring and ever-hovering, doing her best to help me get well. The presence of her children, Jack and Annie were both a joy and a welcome distraction.

In June 1997, a phone call from my daughter-in-law informed me that Tom Hodgins had died of a massive heart attack in Dalton, Georgia at the age of 49. He was to be buried from St. Rose

Church in Carbondale in two days.

Tom had been "on the lam" from the Lackawanna County Courts jurisdiction where there was a warrant for his arrest on non-support charges for his many children. He and his newest wife, along with her five children, had fled to Georgia. On the morning of the funeral, I attempted to view the mortal remains before the family arrived. I needed to know that this sad example of son, husband, and father was really dead. I had to see it with my own eyes.

Mortified to see Tom's mother, Ann Nelson standing in the doorway as I approached the funeral home, she hurriedly put her arms around me and said, "Only you know what I feel now." She then escorted me into the funeral parlor, where she stated, as did his wife, "Tom always loved Anne."

There he was, dead in his coffin and I said a prayer as I stared at him with my stomach in knots. I thought about what profound sorrow this creature had caused me and my family, and I wondered if he was finally at the feet of his God receiving judgment? I stood at the back of the church during his funeral and silently railed at a society which could offer him the finality of a Catholic Mass. I begged God to help me to understand. This man had defrauded hundreds of people, lied, cheated, murdered, deceived and married women without benefit of divorce. He had tortured animals and started fires in the neighborhood during his youth, yet here he was, being given a Christian mass of burial.

I had long ago forgiven Tom—for one cannot survive with a heart full of hate—and in truth, all I felt at that moment was tremendous relief that he could no longer wreak his devastation on others. I hoped that he was finally standing before God to receive his true sentence. I wondered if he had changed at all during the course of his life and later discovered he had not. He had stood trial at least eighteen times for various crimes and served time in prison.

That summer Andy bought a paddleboat, and we faithfully took rides around the lake in the evening, not only for the exercise but also the solitude. With the motorboats silenced, the evenings were quiet, and we especially savored those times together. Unable to be alone at the cottage because of my knee surgery until mid-July, we spent only weekends there.

On July 23, 1997, during a most memorable paddleboat ride and as we watched one of the most glorious sunsets over the mountains, Andy turned to me, and asked, "Will you marry me?"

When I recovered from the shock—for we had courted for fourteen years—I replied, "I guess so."

Returning to shore, we planned a wedding for August 29, 1997, and at 11:30 a.m. on that sunny, beautiful Friday, we were married in St. James Church by Monsignor Peter Owens with my sister, Aileen and Andy's father, Elmer, attending us. As I waited in the rear of the church, on the arm of my brother-in-law, Russell, my favorite musician, Jan de Angelo rendered "Pachelbel's Canon," prior to the ceremony, and sang the "Ave Maria" at

Communion.

Having planned the wedding in one month, I was relieved it went off without a hitch. Family and friends whom we loved were there and the priest who had accompanied us to Ireland performed the ceremony. I, in my pink chiffon dress and carrying a white bible, and Andy, in his blue pin-striped suit and bow tie, were exceedingly happy. During the ceremony, however, after we'd exchanged vows and rings, Monsignor asked if we'd forgotten something. I thought to myself, "Oh, no, what have I forgotten," and realized what it was when Andy suddenly swept me into his arms and kissed me! The whole congregation laughed.

Despite the fact that I'd had knee surgery three months prior, I was able to dance with Andy at the reception at Endwell Greens. Afterward, my children, my sisters and their husbands came to the house to visit where we had a pizza party and played games. At one point, Andy raised a few eyebrows when he asked me, "What are we going to do on our wedding night?" Although our guests didn't know it, I knew he was questioning whether we'd go to the cottage or remain in New York!

A week later, we flew to the Bahamas for our honeymoon. We swam in the Olympic sized pool, ate at the barbeques provided by the club, played cards, shopped, and enjoyed nightclubbing with the beautiful Bahamian natives singing and dancing the "Limbo." We also struck up a friendship with another couple, Bill and Jocelyn Woods, who'd also married that year.

Arriving home, we then motored to Branson, Missouri, where we attended fabulous shows by the Osmond Brothers, Charley Pride, and Bobby Vinton. We even danced onstage to the Glen Miller Orchestra. Bill and Jocelyn Woods, who we had met in the Bahamas drove into Branson from their home on the outskirts and joined us for dinner and a show. After a week in the Ozarks we attended the annual hardware show in St. Louis, and took a cruise down the Mississippi, on the "Becky Thatcher." We ate at the only McDonald's on a ship in the Mississippi.

Being retired, however, time often hung heavy on my hands. I read avidly, volunteered, sewed for the grandchildren and compiled *A History of Vandling*, a book which celebrated the town's Centennial in 1999. I discovered I enjoyed writing, a pleasure I'd intended to embark on at some point in my life.

After a point, I told Andy I would work a few hours at his hardware store, but since neither hardware, computers, nor figures, were familiar to me, I found this to be a distinct challenge!

In early 1999, I traveled to Augusta, Georgia alone, to accompany my daughter Aileen into the delivery room when she gave birth to her daughter Ashlynne. Upon my return home, in February, Andy announced that he was "selling the hardware store and retiring."

For nine months, he hoped a realtor could sell it, but no one came to either inspect or buy it. In July 2000, he began liquidation, a long, tedious, and heartbreaking procedure. To see the fruit of his twenty-one years in business literally being given away, was a soul-wrenching process. Still, the many people who praised his inestimable help, patience, and extreme business accomplishments over the years heartened me. So many lamented the loss of his small business in their neighborhood, telling us, "We could always come to Endwell Hardware where we got true personal service." Unfortunately, the coming of the "Big Boxes" into many towns, has meant the demise of many small businesses, but Andy takes everything with equanimity. "One day at a time," he says. He had left everything in God's hands, working as hard as he could to clear out all the inventory he had acquired in the past twenty years. On February 17, 2001, a final auction was held and Andy retired.

Each time these life changes occurred, Anne was never far from my thoughts. I was so proud when her daughter, Amy completed her college curriculum in December 2000, and received her degree in psychology with a perfect average. Amy was rearing her daughter, Brianna alone and working while studying, but she had achieved a goal I considered almost insurmountable. As she stepped onstage to accept her diploma, tears welled in my eyes, and I could feel Anne's presence, saying "I am so proud of you!"

When the ceremony was over and Amy came offstage, she rushed over to me and said, "Gram, I could feel her standing beside me." I nodded my head and hugged her, and then the two of us wept.

EPILOGUE

In the ensuing years, after I finished this book, life had a way of repeating itself. Marriage to Andrew is and was a great decision, for we have enjoyed many wonderful times together: the opera, symphony, travel, and times with my children, at the cottage, at their homes, and at mine. Andrew truly enjoys gardening at both places, and I spent a lot of time making quilts for the babies and newlyweds, volunteering at the hospital, singing with different groups, and finally, at age 79, taking up the harp! Nancy said I should have taken up the kazoo, since it's far more portable, but Andrew doesn't mind packing it up for transport. I have to admit, there were a few times when we looked like Frick and Frack trying to put the cover on it, but after studying it and calculating that the zipper ran down the front it has become a forty-second job!

We joined the Senior Citizen group in Endwell, and I found new friends in the Newcomers' group. We often play canasta, go to lunch and movies, and have book club discussions, as well as social—and eating—nights. Andy and I often stopped off at the coffee hour after Mass, and deliberately sat with new people so that we could become friendly with more faces at church.

One of the saddest things for me is that, unfortunately, now approaching our winter years, too many funerals have become a part of our lives. We have had to say goodbye to loved ones, friends from our childhood and training days, and many of those from the early years of our lives. One of the most traumatic of these was the passing in 2014 of my dear friend, Carol, with whom I'd shared so much over the past thirty-two-years. We'd become friends in 1982 when we carpooled together, driving every week to the B.C. Pops' practices. Our conversations during those drives instilled a deep friendship which evolved into weekly phone calls to "vent" about our troubles and give an ear to the good times and hard times of those years. Our lives resembled one another's—we each had eight children—and cemented our friendship. We both loved to talk—and could to a stone—and our strange senses of humor carried us through many experiences.

As the years went by, both Carol and I had our physical problems. She ended up having a gall bladder operation, while I underwent three knee replacements, open heart surgery and having stents inserted in my coronaries, but we were always there to support each other. However, when Carol later had to have a hip replacement, she never seemed to rally. She suffered debilitating depression—she had always been the care-giver and felt unhappy being idle—and her health didn't seem to return. By 2014, I noticed that our lunch dates were further and further apart and when I would stop by to see her she was always dressed in her oldest clothes, couldn't walk very far and complained often of being chilly. As a nurse, I pondered what could be wrong. I knew she was seeing five different doctors that summer.

Eventually, Carol told me she was diagnosed with a

"carcinoma."

"A carcinoma of what?" I asked, but she couldn't tell me. All she knew was that she was having repeated MRI's, CT scans, and blood tests.

I was spending a lot of time at the cottage then so we didn't communicate as frequently, but I couldn't believe the doctors could not give her a diagnosis. Finally, in spring of 2015, her son started looking at assisted living arrangements for his mother, but Carol resisted. Eventually, however, she gave in and agreed to a place called Ideal Living. She and her husband would have to sell the house, of course, and Carol appeared very unhappy, often crying for no reason.

Although I knew something was wrong with my dear friend, no one could tell me what, and I puzzled over trying to figure it out. I did my best to cheer her up, but nothing seemed to work. One day that summer, Carol called me and told me that the doctors decided that she had sarcoidosis, an auto-immune disease that Andy occasionally suffers from. Sarcoidosis is non-fatal, however, and Carol appeared to be failing by the day. Stopping by to see her one day, I was shocked to see how much she had deteriorated. She rarely left the house anymore, claiming that she didn't feel well enough to go out, and I noticed that she now suffered from tremors and had a hard time getting about.

That June, we moved down to the lake as usual and shortly after, Carol's daughter called to tell me they had put her mother in Willow Point Nursing Home. I immediately made arrangements to see her that week and was startled to find her curled in a fetal position in the dark room which had the drapes drawn and the door closed. Carol, I realized, was barely able to sit up. When her lunch came, she refused it and then wept as she told me about the room, the food and the care. I noticed that under the bed were two mismatched shoes, and I commented about them. Carol just fluffed it away with the wave of a hand.

"Oh, Don," she said, as though that was all she could expect.

Eventually I paid Carol six visits, and with each one I noticed she was more and more depressed. She wasn't eating, and was growing weaker by the day. She was unable to do the physical therapy no matter how much the girls tried to encourage her and I was distressed to find that no one was ever there when I visited her.

During the last week of August, Carol called to tell me she was at Lourdes Hospital. I immediately made a trip up to see her, and when I walked in the room I was shocked to find her lying flat on her back, dozing. She was clean and comfortable, but images of Stan swirled through my head. He had been at Lourdes when he was dying too.

There was an nun sitting at a desk working on her computer which I found odd. When I asked what she was doing there, she replied, "This is my mission," and I realized that Carol had someone in the room with her twenty-four hours a day.

"Was this Hospice Care?" I asked myself, but there was no

one there to give me an answer. I knew then that Carol was not going to last long and I told her how much she had meant to me and that I loved her dearly. She told me that she loved me, too. I left the hospital that day with a heavy heart and that night, Carol's daughter called to tell me that she was going into hospice for "comfort care." I realized then that I had probably seen Carol for the last time.

On Sunday, August 30, at 9:00 a.m. in the morning, the phone rang beside the bed and I picked it up with great trepidation. It was Carol's daughter who told me, "Mom passed away last night with the family surrounding her."

It was Labor Day weekend, and I was facing another loss of someone I loved. Because of the holiday, the family planned a service for Monday at the funeral home, and after the viewing I felt awful. Carol had been an ever-practicing Catholic, but there had been no Mass. According to her children, that had been "to spare Dad," but it seemed so wrong to me. Carol had dutifully taken all her children to Mass every Sunday. She loved her religion, and it seemed so disrespectful to have no final farewell at the church.

Months later, I learned that Carol had died from Non-Hodgkin's Lymphoma, and I asked her husband when they had been told about this final diagnosis.

"In July," he answered.

I wondered if Carol had been told, and doubted that she had. I'm a firm believer that patients should be made aware if their days are numbered. I couldn't help but wonder if this was why Carol cried so much; because she had no one to air her feelings to about her impending death. Surely, she must have suspected. I sometimes wonder if families and doctors think that by not telling a patient about their true medical condition they are sparing them. I know from my nursing career that they are not. People want to know. They have affairs to put in order, things they need to say, and people they want to see. Doctors and families should not rob them of these things.

Carol's death was devastating to me, as once again it forced me to face my own mortality. When I think about all that has transpired in my life, I realize that it has been filled with heartbreak and tragedy, but good times too, and I know I am truly blessed. I have Andy and my children and my grandchildren. All of them are happy and healthy for the most part. I have Amy too, so much like my lost daughter. I have more than many, and have suffered less than others. But sometimes, when I'm at the cottage with the lake shimmering in the moonlight and a gentle breeze drifting softly through the trees, I think about Anne and Stan. All those memories; of the good times and the bad, of funny moments, stressful situations, arguments, tears and laughter. The memories are bittersweet, because they both have missed out on so much. I find the tears come easy when I think about that, because Anne and Stan should be here and they're not.

The Nightingale Sings

Anne Crowley

CPSIA information can be obtained
at www.ICGtesting.com
Printed in the USA
LVHW032146190319
611218LV00001B/153/P